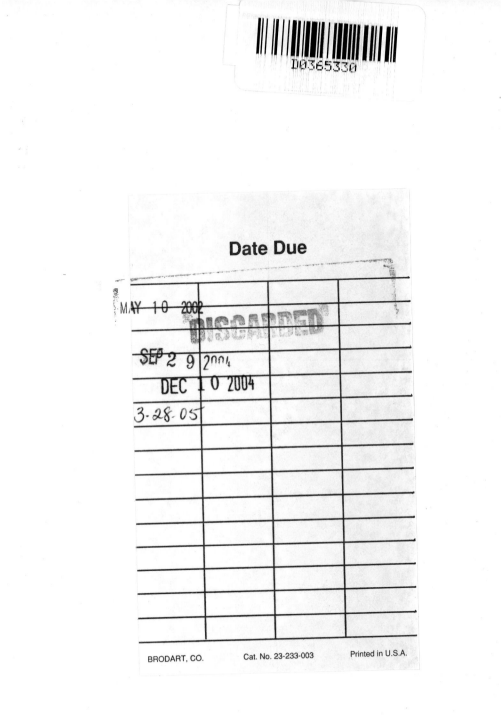

Date Due

BRODART, CO.   Cat. No. 23-233-003   Printed in U.S.A.

OUTSOURCING IT – THE LEGAL ASPECTS

Outsourcing IT – The Legal Aspects

Rachel Burnett

© Rachel Burnett 1998

Published by
Gower Publishing Limited
Gower House
Croft Road
Aldershot
Hampshire GU11 3HR
England

Gower
Old Post Road
Brookfield
Vermont 05036
USA

Rachel Burnett has asserted her right under the Copyright, Designs and Patents Act 1988 to be identified as the author of this work.

British Library Cataloguing in Publication Data

Burnett, Rachel
    Outsourcing IT – the legal contract
    1. Information technology – Management 2. Electronic data processing departments – Contracting out 3. Information technology – Law and legislation 4. Electronic data processing departments – Contracting out – Law and legislation
    I. Title
    658.4'038011

    ISBN 0-566-07698-5

Library of Congress Cataloging-in-Publication Data

Burnett, Rachel.
    Outsourcing I. T. : the legal aspects / Rachel Burnett.
        p.   cm.
    Includes bibliographical references.
    ISBN 0-566-07698-5
    1. Computer contracts--Great Britain.   I. Title.
    KD1642.C65B87   1998   97-47695
    343.7309'99--dc21   CIP

Typeset in 11pt Palatino by Photoprint, Torquay, Devon and printed in Great Britain by MPG Books, Bodmin.

Contents

Foreword

From one point of view, 'outsourcing' information systems and technology is little more than another name for a well established practice. No commercial computer users have designed and built their own computers since Lyons built the Lyons Electronic Office (LEO) for their famous Tea Shop system more than 40 years ago. On one analysis what we now call 'outsourcing' is just a continuation of a trend.

What makes outsourcing in the sense used in this book so different and so complex? To a professional information systems practitioner, several features stand out.

One is the large number of eggs in one basket. The tendency to bundle the development of systems and/or the provision of software with the operation and updating of a service exposes customers to peculiar potential risks.

Another is the risk of being locked into indefinite dependence on a supplier, even when the original contract has run its course, and the difficulty of changing suppliers if the service is poor or the relationship has broken down.

Yet another is the comprehensive and complex nature of the deal. The ideal of a contract whose terms unambiguously anticipate and provide for every conceivable eventuality is totally unrealistic for transactions of this kind. Differences in expectations, understanding and interpretation between the parties will inevitably occur. The trick is to have a means of resolving them before they develop into disputes.

To compound all that, the deal may deprive customers of direct control over their information systems strategy supporting their business and leave them without access to the professional competences needed to manage and negotiate with suppliers.

All these issues, and others which must not be ignored, such as intellectual property arrangements, the complexities of transferring staff, property and other assets, tendering procedures and performance monitoring are dealt with by this book. Its scope is rather modestly expressed as the key factors involved in the legal agreement. In fact, the prospective agreement forms the focus to identify and discuss a comprehensive range of topics with a degree of insight which is music to the ears of an information systems engineer.

No one who is not prepared to think hard about, and think through, all the issues raised in this book should contemplate outsourcing IT. Thinking them through and collecting and analysing all the data they demand will, however, be a most beneficial exercise for any organization, even if it does not ultimately proceed with outsourcing.

The advice in this book should be welcomed by suppliers, too, as counterparties to outsourcing contracts. Well planned and well structured outsourced assignments, from well informed and well advised customers are much more likely to be satisfactory to suppliers.

It is clear from Rachel Burnett's comprehensive treatment of this topic that the parties to outsourcing contracts need access to very well informed and competent legal advice. I believe that it also becomes clear that, in many cases, the creation and subsequent operation of these contracts requires reliance on support analogous to the role of the independent consulting engineer in other fields, to ensure smooth and fair operation, to facilitate the rapid resolution of differences and to provide a

means of managing the changes and evolutionary developments which are inescapable in such a dynamic field of
endeavour.

In sum, this book lays an excellent foundation for an
understanding of how to progress to successful outsourcing
and none of its contents can safely be disregarded.

Ron McQuaker
Exxel Consultants Limited
(Past President of the British Computer Society 1996/7)

Preface

Outsourcing has been described as 'one of the big issues of the decade for the computer industry'* and this book is about the principal features which should be considered in drawing up and managing contracts for outsourcing information technology and information systems. Its purpose is to help business managers to understand the key factors involved in the legal agreement, both for organizations which are considering outsourcing and for organizations which provide outsourcing.

I hope that I have made the main legal issues associated with outsourcing accessible to readers who may never have had to consider them before, and reinforced the messages for those who have.

A legal contract should set out what has been agreed between the parties, covering all the elements of the arrangements which matter. It should never be treated as something separate and unrelated to business reality which is signed for respectability and subsequently ignored. The discussions which take place in negotiating the details of the terms and conditions may well

* Peter Griffiths, then Group Marketing Director of Hoskyns, quoted in the *VAR Journal*, March 1992.

raise matters which had not initially been considered. The resulting decisions will benefit the long-term relationship of the parties in clarifying the nature of the arrangements and promoting the commercial success of the transaction.

As this is intended to be a practical book for IT managers, references to statutes or case law are made only as appropriate to indicate my sources where this may be useful, not to give authority for every statement as would be done for an academic text. Chapter 15 amplifies the references and books mentioned. It should also be noted that the discussions in the book proceed on the basis of the legal jurisdiction of England and Wales.

I am very fortunate to have had sound advice from a number of colleagues. Iain Monaghan, a partner at Masons, and Angela Cha, a senior associate, both of whom have great experience in outsourcing transactions, have made valuable comments on the draft from a legal perspective. I have taken into account the helpful observations on the technical aspects, style and read-ability made by Eur. Ing. Richard Sizer, a colleague on the BCS Security Committee. My thanks go to Hilary Norris for com-menting on Chapter 4 from her knowledge of public procure-ment, to Christine Kiernan for assistance on EU law matters relating to Chapter 8 and to Luan Kane for his expert guidance on the thorny complexities of transfer of staff discussed in Chapter 7.

I am most grateful to Ron McQuaker for his thoughtful critique of the text. I have taken advantage of his remarks concerning the following in particular: independent profes-sional evaluation and standards; the analogy between out-sourcing and the supply of utility services; assessing the supplier's response; the distinction between 'disputes' and 'differences'.

Finally I would like to thank Gwen Clarke for her general secretarial and administrative support.

Nevertheless, I should make it clear that, as I have not incorporated every suggestion or modification proposed, any remaining infelicities survive despite, not because of, all the help I have received.

Rachel Burnett

Abbreviations

Generally speaking, these terms are quoted in full on their first occurrence and subsequently by their abbreviated form.

ADR   Alternative Dispute Resolution
BCS   British Computer Society
CEDR   Centre for Dispute Resolution
CSSA   Computing Software and Services Association
DTI   Department for Trade and Industry
EC   European Commission
ECU   European Currency Unit
EU   European Union
ISO   International Standards Organization
IT   information technology
ITSEC   IT Security Evaluation and Certification Criteria
NCC   National Computing Centre
PC   personal computer
SCL   Society for Computers and Law
TED   *Tenders Electronic Daily*
TUPE   Transfer of Undertakings (Protection of Employment) Regulations 1981
UCTA   Unfair Contract Terms Act 1977
VAT   value added tax

1   Introduction

Expenditure by companies and other organizations on outsourcing information technology (IT) continues to increase.
Lessons are now being learned to counteract the unbridled
enthusiasm with which some of the early outsourcing deals
were concluded, in many cases with a careless, even reckless,
disregard for contract provisions which would have clarified
such matters as the extent of the services, service levels,
charging rates and how long the agreement should last.

An outsourcing contract can be a complex and intricate
contract to draft and negotiate, having precise and objective
criteria for measuring what is to be delivered and paid for, to
the benefit of both parties, with particular methodologies
applied to levels of service and formulae for payment.

Managers in organizations paying for outsourcing and in
businesses offering outsourcing should be fully conversant with
the scope and the essential details of the transaction which
has been agreed, by means of a contract document which will
help them in working together to make the arrangement a
success.

Definitions

In this book the terminology 'supplier' and 'customer' will be used throughout, for consistency and simplicity, to identify respectively the company providing the outsourcing services and the company or other organization paying for the services. Other terms frequently used are 'vendor' or 'provider' for the former and 'client' or 'user' for the latter.

The term 'outsourcing' is taken to mean contracting out defined activities or services by a customer to a supplier to manage and run to agreed standards over an agreed period of time. It may encompass the transfer to the supplier of the customer's staff and/or fixed assets and/or premises used in the provision of the services.

The terms 'facilities management' and 'outsourcing' are often used synonymously. Conversely, they may be found to be distinguished in use in diametrically opposed ways. Both concern the provision of services in a particular way, but then usage varies according to the kinds of services, whether management is involved, whether development is concerned, whether it is wholesale service management or only part. *Facilities management* may generally be categorized as pertaining to a facility or a system which is run externally by a third party for the customer organization. *Outsourcing* is generally understood to include management of the services contracted out, and sometimes their further development, to specific standards.

Because outsourcing is a fashionable term in common use, it is also often applied rather inaccurately to situations which are not about contractual commitments to service levels, but which concern the provision of resources for a development project, or where specialist skills in limited supply are called for to meet a specific purpose, or where the arrangement is simply for support and maintenance by a third party.

Trends

The UK outsourcing market is continuing to grow, however the definition is applied. One survey published in 1997 shows that outsourced IT represents 20 per cent of UK IT external expenditure – or approximately £92 million – although the growth slowed down from 55.6 per cent in 1996 to 11.6 per cent in 1997.[1] The total value of new contracts awarded in 1996 was £357 million, compared with £545 million in 1995.[2]

The indications are of increased growth both in the UK and in Europe, predicted at 15–20 per cent per year for the rest of this decade[3] – a growth more rapid than in any other sector in the software and services market. Central government is the largest and still a fast-growing spender, followed by the utilities, financial services and manufacturing. IT budgets are rising for external services more than for staff or software, or for hardware as the cost of processing power declines.

The development of outsourcing

As recently as 30 years ago only the largest companies and parts of the public sector owned computers and employed cohorts of analysts and programmers. Their machines were large stand-alone mainframes taking up vast areas of load-bearing floor space and were used for the automatic processing of massive volumes of data. The important contracts in data processing were for the purchase of hardware from the computer suppliers. By comparison, software contracts were rare.

The basic software to run the machines arrived 'bundled' with them. Almost all application systems comprised suites of programs individually specified and coded, including those routines needed for every system, such as sorting and printing, whether the systems were for number-crunching, for other office activities or were specially devised for a company's unique requirements.

It has always been common practice, then as now, for a business to commission external contractors to assist with the analysis and programming work. Large companies might give themselves some flexibility by employing temporary staff, in cases where they were unsure of their ongoing work volumes or where they needed additional specialist expertise which was unavailable on a permanent basis. Smaller companies which were unable to justify the capital investment to create their own computing facilities, and other companies of all sizes who saw no need for major capital IT investment, used external bureau services which could run systems off-site. Contracts for the work to be done by independent contractors, or by bureaux, would therefore centre on the operational computer system being run, the number of resources required or the hours individually worked.

As the functions of the departments responsible for computing were transformed from processing reams of data into managing information technology, it continued to be difficult to procure sufficient in-house expertise on a permanent basis. The development of new systems and the acquisition of novel technology were risky undertakings, with constant shortages of skilled and experienced resources. The mainframe bureau service and the supply of contractors and programming resources adapted. Software houses, system integrators and management consultancies expanded, undertaking software development, providing services as required, and agreeing to run the implemented systems. Third-party maintenance and support services grew. The use of external facilities management became a way of keeping a company's moribund machines going, or of managing systems known to have a limited life, while internal staff were redeployed on work which would enhance their own career development and their employer's corporate knowledge base, by installing a new computer or developing the replacement software. Gradually, more services were sent outside, including management tasks, and closely defined results began to be demanded. Ultimately, this might extend to the whole IT and management services departments. Assets and staff being used to provide services in-house would be transferred to the supplier and the services bought back, the supplier using its own assets and staff. Outsourcing had thus become strategic, and its methodology had been refined. Services had to be perceived as adding value for the customer.

Outsourcing has therefore evolved to cover a range of services, from specific tasks or selected projects to complete processes. It may be preceded by the development and implementation of the system which is to be outsourced.

The simplest kind of facilities management contract is at the lowest level of value-added data processing service for transaction outsourcing, such as batch processing for payroll. Another popular option is for existing IT operations – the technical services, maintenance and support, mainframe/data centre or network management, PC support and help desks – to be run externally. This may take place either at the supplier's or at the company's site, leaving the customer with the more interesting work of running its applications and systems development.

The next stage is outsourcing the existing applications, the supplier undertaking their management, maintenance and support, problem-fixing, system enhancements and installation of software upgrades and new versions. The supplier may take responsibility for running systems which it has itself specified, designed, coded and implemented. This is where the customer is more vulnerable and potentially more under the supplier's control, especially where the applications relate to the customer's core business.

Services in which specialized knowledge is at a premium may be outsourced, such as telecommunications, which is characterized by much international regulation and high levels of innovation. Solving the 'Year 2000' problem, by modifying software so that it will continue to work accurately with dates before and after 1 January 2000, is another service requiring narrow expertise which is being outsourced.

In transformational outsourcing, the external supplier maintains existing applications, but moves to new platforms and develops new systems, changing the nature of the customer's IT.

The whole management services function may be outsourced, rather than selected IT activities or services. Those which hit the headlines are the 100 per cent outsourcings of entire IT departments of major organizations, such as the privatization in 1994 of all the Inland Revenue's IT operations to EDS at an original estimate of £1 billion, over ten years, in combination with the system development of the major tax reform of self-assessment. Since then, it has been reported that the price has increased to £1.6 billion.[4]

Meanwhile IT-related contract formats and contents have been changing in order to accommodate these developing business practices. It is essential to have contract provisions which are appropriate for the kinds of outsourcing services being supplied.

The business environment

This process of outsourcing part or all of the IT function is part of an overall shift in business philosophy. The prevailing trend is a move from production to consumption. The tendency is to buy in, not to create from scratch.

In the 1980s the political doctrine of privatizing public sector services began to be put into effect. Government shareholdings in private businesses such as Jaguar and BP were sold. The process continued with the privatization of state-owned businesses such as British Telecom and the utilities.

Attention turned to the public sector. Policy-making was separated from the executive functions of the civil service. Agencies were created and market-testing programmes were formulated for contracting out different kinds of services.

Privatization and contracting out have not, however, been confined to the public sector. Manufacturing, banking and finance, and insurance account for more than half the outsourcing market.

The European legislative context

At the same time as these policies were taking effect in the UK, the European Commission (EC) was implementing legislation to help achieve its objective of an open market. Those EC Directives which concern the procurement of services in the public sector, discussed in Chapter 4, and about the transfer of staff, the subject of Chapter 7, directly affect outsourcing. Directives are rules which are made by the EC to establish policy throughout the European Union. Each member state must implement Directives into its national laws. In the UK this is done by means of primary legislation, Acts of Parliament, or through secondary legislation, statutory instruments or 'Regulations'.

The business approach to outsourcing

In many companies, the directors see IT and its associated services as a high cost and a major frustration in practice. Attracting and retaining good-quality experienced IT staff is a problem, and staff costs are high. Despite falling technology prices, distributed processing and downsizing generally, the costs never seem to come down sufficiently to please the finance director. New system requirements, constant techno-logical innovation and continuous adaptation of software by means of modifications, enhancements and upgrades ensure that change is endemic.

With outsourcing there is a move from fixed, but increasing, internal costs to costs which can be negotiated in advance with competing suppliers. These costs may initially appear to be less expensive. They will be assessed differently from the calcula-tion of the costs of running IT in-house, and they may consequently seem to offer more certainty in their rates and greater flexibility in the choice of what to pay for. Outsourcing is therefore often perceived by a Board of Directors as being an immediate route to operational cost savings – a superficially attractive perspective which is not necessarily justifiable in the long term. Decisions on outsourcing should always take the quality of service into account along with any perceived savings over the expected lifetime of the outsourced activity.

What to outsource

Outsourcing can be seen as a way of freeing the customer organization's management for business management rather than IT function management. There is, however, a view that IT which is critical to a business should not be entrusted to a third party.

Many organizations are dependent on IT for their very existence, but not all of their IT applications will be equally critical.

In justifying the validity of outsourcing as a business approach, the supply of utility services is often used as an analogy. For example, services essential to the running of an organization such as water, electricity or gas are almost always contracted out, yet there is never any concern about the wisdom of doing so. The argument is that, if IT services are viewed simply as a utility function, then the provision of that function by external contractors need be no greater a risk than the provision of any other utility service.

However, such an argument ignores the information content of the IT service. Moreover, the set-up and operation of the machine tools driven by electricity, or the specification and control of the chemical processes fed by water or fired by gas, are not handed over to the utilities.

Nevertheless, a valid distinction can be made between back office systems which may involve extensive volume processing and systems which are at the heart of an organization's intrinsic business processes. At one extreme, payroll is an example of a system where the application of regulations and legislation is common across industries, differing in the details but not the principles, and not mission-critical – unless an organization is in the business of marketing payroll systems. Whether computerized or not, payroll systems have often been handled for a business by external bureau services which can adapt their standard packages to the requirements of an individual company and manage the legislative, procedural, financial and tax changes across the board.

At the other end of the spectrum, IT is also used by an organization to differentiate in its marketplace the way it does business, such as a unique state-of-the-art point-of-sales system for a high street retailer, to give competitive advantage in its core competence. In this context, the use of IT in a dynamic business environment is part of the management of change and the analogy with utility services is much more difficult to uphold. In these cases there is a greater risk that outsourcing may prove to be a disappointment.

Thus, is the IT to be outsourced regarded as similar to a utility function or as a market differentiator? How well established is IT within the outsourcing company's culture? However, in taking this perspective, a simplistic approach must be avoided in assessing the issues of allocation of risk and limitation of liability to be set out in the contract.[5] Business conditions change, and great care must be taken in evaluating the risks of outsourcing IT and information systems activities of long-term significance, such as strategic planning, information resource management, decision support systems, strategic applications planning and business analysis. The risk that the customer inadvertently abandons control of a key resource to external suppliers must be minimized.

In these circumstances, the customer should be asking itself questions about its business objectives and philosophy in order to justify its decision on outsourcing – for example:

- What parts of IT would be suitable for contracting out? Can they be characterized as routine operations or are they business differentiators?
- How will outsourcing fit in with the overall business direction?
- What benefits are being sought? Are these realistic?
- Might security be compromised?
- How will success be measured?
- Is it the right time to consider outsourcing? For example, is a new IT or business strategy to be introduced in the foreseeable future?

- How will its information systems be controlled or exploited?
- Where will innovation, whether technological or in information systems, originate?

Reasons to outsource

The decision to outsource should be taken for sound business reasons. It should not be driven by technological considerations or by costs savings alone. Even if financial reasons may lie behind the move to outsourcing, they should not be the sole long-term objective.

Positive reasons for outsourcing are:

- to limit uncertainties by predicting costs (where this is feasible)
- to focus in-house resources on more strategic business issues or on new technology and systems
- to reduce IT management time spent on recruitment, budgeting, administration and selection of technology
- to gain access to new technologies and skills – perhaps on the basis of economies of scale, in that suppliers can acquire the latest technology by spreading the costs over a number of customers, whereas it can be difficult for an individual customer to justify the continuous application of up-to-date technology for itself
- to improve business efficiency by buying in a more systematic approach to service provision.

Structure of the book

The chapters which follow each concentrate on different aspects of the outsourcing contract.

The structure and format of the contract are discussed in Chapter 2. Commentators on outsourcing all emphasize the importance of the contract in the outsourcing transaction. The planning for outsourcing and the timescale allowed must allow time for contract drafting and negotiating. It is easy to under-estimate the level of detail to be taken into account when decisions have to be taken.

The customer's choice of supplier should be made carefully. This is the theme of Chapter 3. For simple outsourcing, a single person may be responsible. Normally a team representing different interests will be coordinated for this purpose. The expertise may exist in-house or outsourcing consultants may be appointed to advise. At the early stages, the selection processes may be highly confidential. There should be a defined, objective procedure for the selection, and the criteria will include the supplier's financial stability, experience, quality provision, com-patibility and flexibility. Multiple suppliers may be considered, although challenges will arise for the customer in managing more than one supplier.

The selection process for central government, utilities and local authorities is formalized under the public procurement regime as explained at Chapter 4.

Chapter 5 focuses on services and service level agreements – the heart of the contractual relationship and the most import-ant, yet most difficult, part to formulate correctly.

The contract may have to cover the transfer of human resources, equipment and premises. These issues are discussed in Chapters 6, 7 and 8. A complex area of law, driven by European legislation, has developed and continues to evolve in respect of transfer of staff, which cannot be ignored. Software must be correctly licensed. The supplier must be able to run software originally licensed to the customer by third parties. The supplier's use of its own software may cause particular long-term concerns if it creates a dependence by the customer on that software and supplier.

The charges for the outsourcing services may be calculated in a number of ways, outlined in Chapter 9.

Once outsourcing is an accomplished fact, the customer's IT management roles must be adapted. While management will no longer be responsible for running the IT function which has been outsourced, it must still retain some control in order to ensure that the outsourcing arrangement is effective in practice. The customer should no more be able to walk away from the outsourcing of its IT function than it would be able to distance itself entirely from any other important part of its business. Outsourcing failure or success will largely depend on the way it is managed by the customer and on successful liaison between customer and supplier. Cooperation and goodwill, so essential to IT management generally, are vital to outsourcing contracts, but not at the expense of having proper control procedures and objective measurements. Chapter 10 proposes procedures for liaison, which should be set out in the contract. Formal methods for variations to the contract requirements are part of this liaison, as recommended in Chapter 11.

In Chapter 12 the issues of confidentiality, security and reliability are discussed. These will differ in importance from system to system and from customer to customer. Whatever is involved in the particular transaction must be identified and specified in the contract.

The contract will last for a fixed period of time. In its negotiation there is normally a perception of permanence by the customer, that outsourcing is to be a new and continuing process, and that the relationship with the particular supplier chosen will last as far ahead as can be imagined. Nevertheless, there is always the possibility of the relationship coming to an end at some time in the future, whether through the breakdown of the association over time, a clash of management personalities, the financial vulnerability of the outsourcing supplier, a change of business direction on the part of either party, or for other reasons. Chapter 13 describes the options open to the customer, whether the choice is to be contract renewal, a new contract with another supplier or bringing the services back in-house. The consequences must be set out in the contract, so that it is clear what the responsibilities of each party are.

In negotiating for outsourcing, it must always be borne in mind what the objective is to be, what the outsourcing process is expected to achieve, and what enforceability should be incorporated in the contract should any aspect of the transaction go badly wrong. The supplier must limit its liability realistically. The customer will expect some remedies to be available if things do go wrong. This is the subject of Chapter 14.

Chapter 15 concludes by giving an example of an outline contract framework. Finally, some addresses and other references are given.

Notes

1 'Computer Weekly/Kew Associates 1997/UK IT Expenditure by 16 Industry Sectors', quoted in *Computer Weekly*, 10 July 1997.
2 *The Holway Report 1997*, reported in *Computing*, 3 July 1997.
3 Examples of growth predictions: Datamonitor – 19 per cent each year; Frost & Sullivan – 14 per cent a year 1995–98 (quoted by Jenny Mill in *IT Text* **1** (1)).
4 *Computer Weekly*, 17 April 1997.
5 An interesting discussion on this point is by Mary C. Lacity, Leslie P. Willcocks and David F. Feeny in 'IT Outsourcing: Maximise Flexibility and Control', *Harvard Business Review*, May–June 1995.

2 Contract planning, structuring and negotiating

Surveys on the successes and failures of outsourcing emphasize that satisfied customers had signed comprehensive contracts where the issues had been thought through, and dissatisfied customers had not signed contracts which were clear or detailed. As a supplier or as a customer, it is vital to have a properly negotiated contract in writing with the other party to the outsourcing arrangements, covering legal, commercial and service requirements.

In this chapter some points relating to the contract structure are examined. These include the planning necessary before starting to draft the wording, the decisions on the resources to use, the framework for the contents, the philosophy behind it, the law which should apply and other basic formalities.

Broadly, the contract will cover, amongst other things, the services to be provided, the charges, the rights and responsibilities of each side, the management of the contract, the extent of the parties' liabilities, how variations to the services may be made, and how the contract may be brought to an end. There may be separate documents for the transfer of assets or the business, for staff transfer and for the services agreements.

Because the outsourcing arrangement relates to one particular business and organization and also to carefully defined services to be supplied, the contract – which may consist of a series of linked documents – must be tailor-made.

The reasons for having a contract

There are at least three good reasons for formal terms to be drawn up and agreed.

The first is that the contract framework will also serve as a structure for the negotiating process. This will guide discussion and eventually help consensus to be reached, so that both parties to the contract understand what they are agreeing, unambiguously.

The second is that the contract should be a source of reference during the provision of the outsourcing services. It will serve as a working document, detailing information about what has been agreed, such as the charging methods, the reporting procedure or the benchmarks for measuring the service levels which are achieved in practice.

Third, in common with all contracts, is the function of setting out each party's rights and responsibilities clearly so that, in the final analysis, the contract can be enforced if any of the important obligations fail to be carried out and the relationship deteriorates.

For both parties, the objectives of what they are trying to achieve from entering into an agreement for outsourcing need always to be borne in mind. A successful outsourcing contract should accurately reflect in its detail the context of the unique relationship between the supplier and the customer for the purposes of the business objectives of the outsourcing. In other words, the contract document must accurately reflect the individual components of the transaction which the parties believe they have made. This will involve close attention to both operational and technical matters. However, it will be negotiated under the pressures of a deadline where solutions to different perspectives and opinions must be agreed and, under these constraints, it will never be perfect.

The parties to the contract and signatories

Who are the parties to the contract to be? A contract must be between legal entities to be enforceable. Corporations, the majority of which are companies formed under the Companies Acts, and charities, which are companies subject to special regulations, are entitled to make contracts. The Crown and other emanations of the state such as government departments may enter into contracts, as may local authorities. Organizations set up under other statutes – some quasi-public Commissions would fall under this heading – are able to exist legally according to what they are permitted to do under the statute concerned, which would normally allow contracts to be made by them. Individuals and partnerships are also legal persons.

A holding company, as shareholder of its subsidiary company, is nevertheless a separate legal entity from it and cannot, simply because of that relationship, speak for the subsidiary or enter into contracts on the subsidiary's behalf. Similarly, the subsidiary has no legal obligation to act as directed by the holding company. On the contrary, the directors of the subsidiary are required to consider its interests independently and may incur personal liability if they fail to do so.

Sometimes either the supplier or the customer may regard itself as a self-contained organization, yet have no distinct legal identity of its own, being in fact merely an operating division within a larger company. The contract should then be entered into by the main corporate body itself. The company will be the party legally responsible. A statement at the start of the contract can make it clear that the contract is between, say, 'X Company Limited' and 'Headco plc by its Systems Division'. In the body of the contract, the company may be referred to by the abbreviated version of the name with which everyone is familiar, such as 'Systems', or the name by which the division or department is known, if this will make the contract more user-friendly and the rights and obligations more readily comprehensible.

Provided that all the terms of the contract have been agreed, it is not essential under English law that the document be signed. However, it is good business practice to record formally the commitment of each party to the agreement that has been reached, signifying the conclusion of the negotiations. Indeed, the event of signing the contract is often marked as a special occasion with suitable publicity arrangements, photographs taken to record the cordial handshakes, the press release issued, and the first cheque handed over.

The contract should be signed by a representative of each party with the authority to do so. It is not necessary in English law to have witnesses to the signatures for a contract which is not a deed. A deed is a special kind of contract, which is required to be used in certain circumstances, such as where there is no 'bargain' involved between the parties to the contract, for example, when one party makes a gratuitous promise to do something, such as to pay money. Outsourcing contracts do not need to conform to the formalities associated with deeds. However, local authorities and other public organizations may have standing orders requiring their contracts above a certain value to be executed as deeds. If a contract is to be a deed, it must be clear from its contents that it is intended to be a deed, and it must be executed under the corporate common seal or signed on behalf of a company by any person acting under the company's authority. A document signed by a director and the secretary of a company or by two directors of the company and expressed as being executed by the company has the same effect as if executed under the common seal of the company.

The rights and obligations in a contract under English law concern the parties to the contract alone. Others do not derive enforceable benefits or responsibilities directly from the contract. Third parties who are involved in the outsourcing, such as the customer's end users or the supplier's subcontractors, must have their own contracts with the customer or supplier respectively; these may need to mirror the relevant rights and obligations appearing in the outsourcing agreement.

Assignment and novation

Unless there is an express prohibition against assignment in the contract, under English law either party may assign the benefit of the contract to another party. An assignment is the transfer of part or all of the benefits of the contract. The contract remains in effect, but the rights of one party, 'the assignor', such as the supplier's right to payment, may be transferred to another party, 'the assignee'. The assignee may then enforce the payment terms in the contract against the customer. The customer will still be able to enforce the contract against the original supplier, whose obligations of providing services are not transferred through the assignment.

It is normal for the contract to place some restrictions on either party's ability to assign it. A clause prohibiting assignment without the prior consent of the other party to the contract is commonly found. This gives the option of refusal of a proposed new relationship with an unsuitable or undesirable assignee. In practice, a customer may want the right to assign the contract if it is likely that, during the term of the contract, its corporate structure of associated companies should change or if the part of the organization for which the services are being supplied is to be sold off. In this case, the customer might require a clause stating that assignment by the customer to its related companies or to a third party will be permitted. In circumstances in which the assignor is a company within a group of companies and the proposed assignee is another company in that group, assignment may be acceptable to the supplier.

If assignment is to be permitted, a safeguard may be introduced by making the assignment subject to the other party's consent. It may be agreed that this consent should not be withheld unreasonably. This will give an opportunity to examine the financial viability of the proposed assignee company and any previous unsatisfactory relationship between the non-assigning company and the proposed assignee.

Sometimes reciprocity is required in the negotiated assignment provisions, or there may be special reasons for permitting or forbidding assignment altogether.

A 'novation' agreement replaces a contract. This may be desirable if the terms and conditions are being significantly varied, or in a situation where the original parties to the contract agree that a third party should take the place of one of them. The effect of a novation agreement is to extinguish the original contract and create a new one. As a new contract, it should be signed by all three parties – the original parties and the party taking over.

Intention to proceed

Occasionally, the supplier's sales representatives want to obtain an early assurance from the customer that its intent to proceed is serious, especially where it is anticipated that negotiations may be protracted. In this case, a letter of intent may be requested. Other names for documents with equivalent purposes are 'heads of terms', 'heads of agreement' and 'memorandum of understanding'. The language and format of the document are matters of choice. It may be worded as an informal letter or it may be constructed as an intimidating-looking paper. It will set out the intentions of one party or of both and outline any key terms already known.

It should be a matter for careful decision whether such a document is really necessary. It may be of some benefit where it is desirable to keep the Board of either organization informed, to avoid misunderstandings, to clarify the steps to be taken or to flush out major areas of possible contention early. It may be of no advantage where it is requested only because of a sales representative's anticipated commission.

The document will need care in drafting, to avoid unlooked-for obligations and also because it will set the tone for further negotiations, the scope for which should not be unnecessarily constrained. It may not be intended to be legally binding, and it is normally highly advisable that it should not have the status of legal enforceability when the parties are in the early stages of negotiations. The most usual way of indicating this is by using the words 'subject to contract', to show that it is not intended to commit the parties. This is a well understood formula, although not foolproof. Other similar phrases do not have the same conciseness and wide acceptance – for example, terms such as 'subject to Board approval' or 'provisional' or 'awaiting formal contract' may be ambiguous as to whether an enforceable agreement has been made in any respect, and therefore should not be used.

In the drafting of the letter of intent, it is the principles which should be enunciated, not the details. It must be clear that all the statements made will be subject to any third-party involvement, such as the consents required for assignment of software licences. It may be appropriate to suggest a contract timetable. It should also be openly acknowledged that it is not a complete statement of the parties' objectives.

Separately from the letter of intent itself, other agreements preliminary to the contract may be required. If confidentiality is of concern, a binding non-disclosure agreement should be separately made, as will be discussed in Chapter 3. There may be circumstances in which the supplier can request a 'lock-out' agreement, meaning that the customer will not negotiate with third parties for a specified period, perhaps in return for the supplier entering into negotiations with third-party software suppliers or of starting its investigation of the customer's service level requirements.

An 'agreement to agree' is not legally enforceable under English law. There are too many potential escapes.

Planning the contract

A good contract will need careful planning from the early stages of considering outsourcing.

At the stage of inviting tenders, some of the contract criteria will already be known. For example, local authority contracts often have standard provisions about compliance with non-discriminatory legislation. It is advisable to include a contract outline or a basic contract with the invitation to tender. Suppliers themselves will have basic terms on which it is profitable for them to conduct business and may wish to include these as part of their tender responses.

There are different views on what terms should be set out by the customer in the contract attached to the invitation to tender. One opinion held by experienced contract negotiators is that all the terms should be included to which the customer would ideally wish the supplier to be committed. An alternative valid negotiating position is that only those terms which are essential and not negotiable, or which are highly desirable, should be set out in the documentation for the invitation to tender. The rationale for this is to avoid deterring potential bidders by contract requirements which are more idealistic than realistic.

Once the supplier has been selected, the provisions of the contract need to be negotiated and agreed. If the contract is for a large-scale outsourcing, the supplier will need to obtain accurate information about all aspects of the services being outsourced, similar to the process of 'due diligence' which is carried out on the sale of a business. The customer will disclose such matters as: third-party contracts; software licences and support agreements; financial details; insurances; leases; property and other proprietary rights; contractor contracts; employment policies; union affairs; disciplinary issues; and terms of employment. A limited part of this information could be supplied at the stage when the invitation to tender is made, so that suppliers have sufficient knowledge to submit 'educated' bids. However, much will be too sensitive to disclose at this early point, even in the unlikely event of the information being readily available.

Most of this information will need to be included in the contract, incorporated into it or referred to in it. At the outset of negotiations, a substantial amount of detail will not be known and the information will have to be collated. A location which can be dedicated to storing relevant information and copies of documents may be necessary.

Service levels may be already known, but it is far more usual for them to be drawn up and agreed by the parties during negotiations. Occasionally they are not agreed until after the contract formally comes into effect – although this is highly inadvisable from the customer's perspective, and not to be recommended. This will be another time-consuming exercise.

Other decisions which need to be taken will emerge from the discussions taking place during negotiation, such as how much weekly or monthly management liaison there should be.

Generally speaking, there is likely to be an enormous amount of work to be done in gathering and establishing the information required. This exercise may be carried out by the customer alone or with participation by the supplier.

For these reasons, an outsourcing contract will take some time to finalize. It can take several months to sort out the commercial aspects and technical issues as well as the legal requirements. The earlier the process is initiated, the less pressures there will be to take quick decisions just to keep the process moving. Decisions taken impulsively in this way are unlikely to be as sound as those made when there has been time to consider all the surrounding circumstances. There are bound to be differences of opinion and approach, but the earlier these can be aired in an atmosphere where everyone is keen to reach the right outcome, the better the result is likely to be. Any problems which arise should be confronted so that they may be resolved. If they are ignored, they will not go away, and the longer they remain, the more difficult it will become to find solutions. From both the supplier's and the customer's point of view, it makes far more sense to sort out problems and find common ground *before* the contract is signed.

A timetable and plan may be prepared, identifying key target dates and events for the contract negotiation, with dates set for signing the contract and for the outsourcing services to commence. This can be useful to keep up the momentum. However, deadlines are often imposed arbitrarily or for political reasons and, if these are unrealistic in the light of the work that has to be done, the decisions which need to be taken and the consensus that must be reached, they can introduce undesirable stress into the negotiation process. For example, the customer may wish the start of the outsourcing service to coincide with the start of its financial year or from termination of the lease on the computer premises, or the contract may have to be signed before the chief executive goes on holiday. The sales representatives of the outsourcing supplier may have their own compelling reasons for wanting the deal to be struck by the end of a particular quarter.

The resources to use in negotiating

The actress Sandi Toksvig once said that in Equity, the actors' union, at any one time there is about 90 per cent unemployment. So actors' negotiations work along the lines of the director saying to the actors, 'You're going to have to take a pay cut', and the actors close the deal by saying 'Well, all right, then'.[1] Negotiating strategy for outsourcing should be more positive than this, rather, as defined by Mark McCormack, as 'the mediation between competing interests, with an eye towards a mutually profitable, face-saving and, whenever possible, relationship-preserving result'.[2]

Goodwill and integrity on both sides are as crucial in negotiating the contract as in carrying out the services.

The contract will cover matters which are unfamiliar to the average customer's managers and normal legal advisers. In addition, for public authorities and utilities, access to expertise in EU procurement law is necessary, as discussed in Chapter 4. For a large-scale outsourcing contract, professional specialist contract advice should be seriously considered by the customer as part of its investment in outsourcing. An outsourcing legal expert will be experienced in knowing what must be covered, in reflecting the commercial terms in legal language by careful drafting, and in advising on the negotiations. Different organizations will have different styles of making the best use of the expertise, depending on their own preferences, in deciding whether or not there should be a legal presence at all the negotiations, in whether or not to expect lawyers to review every technical IT document and so on. Although any in-house legal advisers will typically not be experienced in handling outsourcing contracts, they will advise on general points of the organization's legal policy and may wish to stay informed on the progress of the contract negotiations.

For a large contract, a small team may be picked to coordinate and progress it, including technical, financial, human resources and legal expertise, perhaps with a core negotiating team backed up by background advisers in specialist areas. The individuals involved in the negotiating need clear roles, a target and a strategy, plus the authority to make most of the decisions without having constantly to refer them and delay the process.

The customer needs demonstrable commitment at Board level. One of the directors may be appointed as the senior member of the coordinating team. There should be at least a direct reporting relationship from the team leader to a nominated director at Board level or its equivalent in a non-corporate organization. If an internal appointment is to be made to the role of customer liaison manager, that person should be involved at an early stage, since that is where the overall responsibility will lie for monitoring and managing the contract and for implementing change.

A narrow legalistic approach is inadvisable because it does not make for a good working relationship and, in any event, it will be impossible to cover every eventuality. However, certain legal obligations do have to be taken into account, such as the duty to consult on behalf of staff, as mentioned in Chapter 7. Records of what was negotiated may have to be kept in order to demonstrate that the correct procurement process was followed, in case of legal challenge by other bidders.

It can be a salutary experience to compare the final contract against early drafts. However, the pressures to conclude negotiations and produce a workable contract usually mean that there is no time to do this. Moreover, the requirements on both sides will be subject to modification and compromise while the negotiations are taking place.

Contract structure

The focus of this book is on the agreement for services; this will cover the scope of the services, the service levels, the pricing and payment. There may be several other related agreements, each a separate contract but mutually interdependent and expressly stated to be so. Thus, business and staff transfer agreements will be necessary if premises and personnel are being transferred or leased. These issues are discussed in Chapters 6 and 7 respectively. If land or buildings are being transferred there will also be property contracts.

There may be separate contracts for individual, but associated, applications or functions, for logically independent services – for example, disaster recovery should some unusual event prevent the normal provision of the services – or for consultancy. There may be a systems development agreement in cases where the outsourcing is to a supplier which will be first developing a new system for its customer and then running it.

One single, bound document may be a tidy but optimistic ambition which is not usually achievable in practice or even advisable. If the contract document consists of a thick bundle of papers, as it may be where there are service level agreements or other schedules or appendices, it will be inconvenient and awkward to try to find a particular provision. One means of organizing the paperwork is to have the principal contract conditions in the main part of the contract and to have all the information which may vary during the course of the arrangement set out in appendices or schedules. Any linked agreements, such as the service level agreements, will logically form part of the overall contract terms and conditions but can be kept physically as separate documents. This will make it easier to refer to change control procedures, how to resolve a dispute, how to conduct the formal liaison meetings, the charging rates or what the service levels should be. It is also likely that those staff who need to know what the contract says will need access only to certain information. For instance, if they need to refer to service levels or to change control procedures, they will not need to know the charging basis or the limits of liability. This contract structure and format will also enable updated conditions to be easily included by replacing the schedule concerned, rather than modifying the whole agreement or having updating riders as separate pieces of paper for the clauses altered.

It may be impossible to envisage every event that might occur and as a consequence to make provision in advance. In some places, the contract may deliberately contain statements of intent, rather than consist at all points of a rigorous record of each party's rights and obligations. It may specify methods whereby decisions should be taken during the course of the provision of the services, such as the procedures for evaluating variations required to the services. Legal exactitude must be tempered by flexibility.

Contract formalities

> ... the double challenge in composing any sort of document: keep it simple, but make it complete. The tension between those two goals is not always easy to resolve.[3]

The formality of the wording is a matter of preference. How far technical terms should be spelt out for the uninitiated, the length of the sentences and the manner in which the legal requirements are stated are, to some extent, unimportant questions of style. The contract should be intelligible to those who need to understand it, in reasonably-sized print and in a format and presentation which, as far as possible, is reader-friendly rather than daunting. From a practical perspective, it is helpful for the pages to be numbered, for there to be a contents page, including a list of the schedules, and for the document to be bound securely so that it does not readily disintegrate. It also is useful for its word-processing file reference to be recorded at some point.

A contract will conventionally commence by setting out the names and addresses of the parties, followed by the 'Recitals', which are summarized statements of the purposes of the contract and perhaps the events leading up to its formation. Many contracts continue with long preambles which are not strictly necessary – for example, recording that the masculine includes the feminine or that the singular includes the plural. This is automatically the case under English law.[4] If the contract consists of a number of related agreements, there should be a statement about which of them is to take precedence in the event of any conflicting terms.

Definitions included in the contract should be for those words or terms whose meanings are specific to the contract and which are used more than once in the body of the contract. Such terms, identified in use by capital initials, will then draw the reader's attention to the fact that they are being used in a particular sense and in a consistent way. The same definitions should apply as far as possible across all the contractual documents and schedules.

Within the contract, there will be numbered clauses or paragraphs, each referring to one aspect of the contract, and each clause may be divided into subclauses. For example, one clause may be headed 'Termination' and its subclauses would consist of the different grounds for termination. Schedules may also contain numbered paragraphs. Schedules themselves are often numbered. However, as it may not be clear at the outset of drafting what subject-matter will be appropriate to include in schedules, it is easier to draft the contract if the schedules are given titles and referred to as such. 'Key Personnel Schedule' is more readily identifiable than 'Schedule 5'. Cross-references to clauses or to schedules should always be carefully checked before the contract is finalized, in order to ensure that all the variations leave the numbering correct.

There need be only one contract document signed by both parties. But if both parties want to hold an original document, there can be two identical contracts, each signed by both parties.

The legal system applicable to the contract, and the procedure for giving notices, are basic provisions included in the contract.

Governing law and jurisdiction

For IT outsourcing services, the offices of the supplier and of the customer often do not need to be in close proximity or even in the same country. Outsourcing services may be carried out in a remote location. Public authorities and utilities are bound to consider any company in the European Union which responds to their advertised invitations to tender and meets the criteria, as discussed in more detail in Chapter 4.

The contract should be drawn up according to one legal system. A clause should be included stating which legal system governs the interpretation of the wording and the operation of the provisions, and which courts are to have jurisdiction should a dispute lead to legal proceedings. If either party is a British company or an organization with an address in England or Wales, a statement can be made to the effect that the contract will be governed and interpreted by the law of England and Wales. The discussions in this book proceed on the basis of this legal jurisdiction.

Notices

If notice should be given to terminate the contract, or notice be given of breach of contract, it is as well to have an agreed formal means of doing so. There will be a clause to specify what is acceptable practice for notices relating to the contract.

The notice must be in writing in order to minimize the scope for dispute. A simple provision would cover notices delivered personally or sent by first-class mail, deemed to be received within two working days, although if one of the parties is located abroad, a longer period would be appropriate. It is possible to include fax, telex or electronic mail, if these are agreed by the parties to be the permitted means of receiving notices and if it is made clear in the contract when the notice will be deemed to have been received.

It is important to be precise and to allow for the rules of different postal systems if the parties do not belong to the same jurisdiction and the laws on notice differ. For example, recorded delivery is useful for evidential purposes within the UK, and there are often equivalent arrangements abroad.

The clause may also state to whom the notice should be addressed, such as the company secretary or the solicitor's department, who will act on it. Job titles are preferable, since they are more permanent than named individuals.

The contract and nothing but the contract

A 'representation' is a legal term used for a statement made by one of the parties before the contract has been agreed. The contract will normally include a provision that neither party has relied on any representations except any which are recorded within the contract, and that nothing written or verbal will be of any effect unless set out in the printed contract or incorporated by inclusion or reference in a schedule or appendix. Specifically, liability will be excluded for pre-contract representations. If this provision is effective, this will give certainty if evidence is ever needed about what terms and conditions went to form the contract.

Each party should scrutinize correspondence, documents, sales brochures, notes of meetings held from the time the parties first began to negotiate, and on which they may wish to rely when the contract is in operation. For example, a letter by the sales director of the outsourcing company, setting out the company's experience with similar-sized companies in the same market area as the customer, might have been important to the customer. A statement made by the customer that it would be increasing its long-term strategic IT expenditure in the area being outsourced may be significant for the supplier.

Ideally, any representation being relied on by either party should be set out in the formal agreement as a term of the contract. Alternatively, a representation may be incorporated by reference to the date of the letter or meeting when the representation was made, if this can be done without introducing ambiguity or the correspondence or note of the meeting concerned can be attached as a schedule to the main agreement.

The exclusion of liability for pre-contract representations is legally permitted only subject to a test of 'reasonableness'.[5] The actual wording and surrounding circumstances would be reviewed carefully in the event of a dispute if the clause were ever to be challenged in the courts. If the contract is a negotiated agreement so that the clause has been positively agreed, and if there is correspondence or there are any notes of meetings or other statements about events which took place before the execution of the contract which are recorded in the contract, it is likely that the clause will be regarded at law as reasonable (subject to an exception if the representation was fraudulent).

A contract can be rescinded or set aside as a result of a misrepresentation on which the other party relied in entering into the contract, if the misrepresentation had been made negligently or even innocently – for example, by a sales representative who honestly believed what he was saying at the time.

If the other party has no reasonable grounds for having made the representation, damages can be claimed by the party not at fault as the amount necessary for that party to be reinstated to the same situation as if the contract had not been made. This is different from the position that the party would have been in had the representation been true. Damages for misrepresentation do not compensate for any loss of bargain or loss of profit. However, if the innocent party can show that it suffered loss as a result of relying on a misrepresentation made fraudulently, then damages may be recovered for that loss.[6]

It therefore makes better sense to include any important commitment made as a warranty term in the contract. The remedy for any breach of warranty is the amount necessary to restore the injured party to the position in which it would have been had the warranty been true. This is preferable as a remedy, as it will normally enable a greater amount of damages to be claimed. (In practice, the figures are often similar.)

In a contract lasting for any length of time there will be adjustments and variations made while the contract is in force. To cater for these, the contract should have a clause permitting variations to the wording to be made under specific circumstances: that they are in writing; dated after the contract date (otherwise, they would conflict with the requirement for everything to be contained in the contract at the time of signature); and signed by both parties to show that the modification has been agreed. There may also be a requirement that the status of the signatories to contract variations should be at the same level as that of the original signatories.

Contract philosophy

A successfully negotiated outsourcing contract should not be hidden away (or worse still, lost) once it has been signed. It should remain available to the people operating and monitoring the outsourcing services, as a source for referring to procedures, parameters and service levels. Not everyone will need to know all the intricacies and complexities, but different features will be relevant to different managers of the contract process.

If the contract is long and complicated with a number of schedules, a user guide to cover the points which will arise day-by-day will be a very useful document. It does not need to cover every aspect of the contract and it should not be in language which is remotely legalistic, but it should be a practical guide to the way in which the agreement works.

However much trust the parties believe they have in working together, this should never be an excuse for the contract requirements not to be properly defined. The business circumstances of either party may alter. Any of the people running the outsourcing day-to-day, the members of the management board or holding company personnel of either the supplier or the customer may move away to different work or to another company. Their successors may lack the original commitment or the knowledge of what had been discussed during the negotiations.

The contract should allow for the different objectives of the supplier and the customer. For the supplier, the contract is a source of income. For the customer, the contract is for the provision of services affecting its business.

The balance of control in monitoring the contract should lie with the customer. This is not to say that, in all circumstances, control will be given to existing managers of the customer organization who were formerly responsible for the IT operation. Although it will often be the case that the customer's IT manager becomes the services manager under the new regime, it may be necessary for the customer to make a new appointment of a services manager or a liaison manager, or to decide to bring in external consultants to manage the process. Nevertheless, the day-to-day outsourcing operation should continue to be monitored and controlled from a strategic point of view by representatives of the customer. For this to be effective, there should be a reporting channel for the customer manager, whether this is an internal or an external service function in the organization, direct to the Board or its equivalent level.

In negotiating the contract there should be mutual respect for the parties' perspectives. The supplier must be able to make a profit. The customer must be facilitated in running its business. It is always helpful to give reasons why a particular require-. ment is needed. This enables consensus to be reached, if necessary by examining other ways of achieving the objective.

If the negotiating process is unsatisfactory and confrontational, each party should review whether the relationship is going to work.

A one-sided contract for outsourcing will benefit neither the supplier nor the customer in the long term. Cooperation is essential to the success of outsourcing.

Notes

1   Quoted in an article in *Good Housekeeping* magazine, October 1995.
2   Mark McCormack (1988), *What They Didn't Teach me at Yale Law School*, Fontana Paperbacks.
3   Ibid.
4   Law of Property Act 1925, section 61.
5   Misrepresentation Act 1967.
6   Ibid.

3 Selecting a supplier

The right choice of supplier is crucial. The selection process will take time, preceding the detailed drafting and negotiation of the contract. The customer should allow for adequate resources and management time at the early stages of planning for the outsourcing bid.

The invitation to the prospective suppliers will often be made before the decision to outsource becomes public knowledge. Assurances that the customer's confidentiality will be respected must first be obtained.

The invitation to tender must be carefully prepared to ensure that the information made available to the tenderers will be sufficient and at an appropriate level of detail to enable them to put forward meaningful bids to demonstrate their competence and suitability, and to price the contract.

The consequences of making the wrong choice of supplier will be highly undesirable, even if a carefully drawn contract can minimize the effects. In the selection process, the various elements of quality, cost, expertise, compatibility and the essential characteristics of the supplier must be carefully assessed.

The potential suppliers will also be investing time, effort and resources in bidding for the work. These will be reduced to one by a process of elimination on the part of the customer. This process should be seen to be conducted fairly and objectively.

While 'partnership' and 'partnering' are terms often quoted – by suppliers rather more frequently than by customers – the outsourcing contract will normally be entered into between the supplier and the customer as independent parties.

Customer preparation

Two early predictors of eventual outsourcing success are clear customer objectives and project sponsorship at a senior level.

One of the customer's early considerations should be whether outsourcing is in fact the most effective method of providing the best services. Would it be practicable to reach the same objective by bringing in experienced project managers or numbers of technically skilled resources on a consultancy or services basis as and when required without any long-term commitment?

Different kinds of outsourcing requirements will appeal to different suppliers according to their expertise. An unambiguous statement of business objectives will help attract the appropriate suppliers. Where the outsourced services proposed by the customer are limited, low in value, and are for routine applications, the supplier's (probably well founded) perception will be that there would be minimal potential for further work in the future. Alternatively, a customer may be wishing to outsource entirely its current IT function prior to the acquisition of new systems and new services which will be developed and provided by the supplier. If the customer will also be demanding business process re-engineering for IT reorganization, this will attract outsourcing suppliers who are more interested in adding value to their services through developing innovative ideas for efficiencies and expansion of the customer's IT needs.

A customer's uncertainty of aims will lead to tender responses which may not be relevant. For example, the original driver for outsourcing may simply be to replace the operational systems. However, several weeks into the selection process, the realization may dawn on the customer that its expectations were set too low, and so it introduces a new requirement of radical technological enhancements. Meanwhile, suppliers have been shortlisted whose expertise lies in running the systems in question, not in evolving new solutions, and the customer will be at risk of making an inappropriate choice of supplier.

Informed discussions within the customer organization should lead to an understanding of what is to be specified in the invitation to tender and what is to be excluded.

It may be appropriate to consider taking the invitation to tender as a two-stage process, the first being the prequalification stage to invite expressions of interest. From these responses, which may vary in the broad solutions proposed, the customer may decide on the particular approach and narrow down the invitation in the second stage to those suppliers who can develop a detailed response according to that approach.

The exploratory stage of learning about the possibilities of the various approaches may therefore be successfully addressed as a separate pre-procurement exercise. Suppliers may be engaged in debate on that basis, and this can provide a legitimate opportunity for them to promote what they can do while various options are still open. This will both assist the customer deciding on the form of outsourcing and may incidentally help identify those suppliers who will be suitable to be invited to make proposals. Following this decision on the form and scope of the outsourcing, a statement of requirements or invitation to tender may be issued and specific responses sought.

This is the time to consider whether the work can be split up. It may not be necessary for the customer to appoint one single outsourcing supplier. It may be less risky to have separate outsourcing functions and have more than one supplier. For instance, the Co-operative Bank has been reported[1] as having four outsourcing arrangements: management of its network of automatic cash machines; credit card processing; cheque-clearing; and development and maintenance of IT systems.

The customer must ensure that there is ownership of, and therefore ultimate responsibility for, the outsourcing contract negotiations through the project sponsorship role. For out-sourcing which is related in any way to a company's business strategy and objectives (in contrast to, for example, outsourcing a self-contained legacy system which will be superseded in a few years), the sponsorship function should be at Board level.

To see the selection process through, a project manager should be appointed, who may be separate from the project sponsor. For large-scale outsourcing, a team of representatives drawn in from all the line functions affected, may assist the project manager. This team may include human resources, estate management, financial management, procurement and possibly a spokesperson for the business end users, to harness their enthusiasm early and to keep them informed.

As a matter of policy, the director of the IT function in the organization ought normally to be closely involved, perhaps as project sponsor if at Board level, or as project manager with responsibility for the management of the outsourcing selection and contract negotiation. There must, in any event, be sufficient professional competence to assess the technical validity and quality of proposals or tenders.

Prospective suppliers should be identified and asked if they would be interested in tendering. Public authorities and utilities have the public procurement regime with clearly laid-down procedures to guide them in the selection process. This is discussed in Chapter 4.

The customer's in-house team may be asked to put in a bid as well. It is important how the bidding process which includes such a bid is managed. Whatever the reasons for considering outsourcing, if the in-house IT team is being given the oppor-tunity to put forward a proposal, their bid must be treated just as seriously as the external bids. Equally, if the exercise is to be undertaken, it must not be a waste of time for the external applicant bidders. There should be an open competitive tender.

If the in-house bid is unsuccessful, the team in place will be suffering a loss of morale, and yet will still be expected to continue working until the time the contract is signed and the supplier takes over. There is a genuine risk here of losing skill and experience through resignations and the customer being left exposed. Thus the shorter the time between the selection of the supplier and commencement of the outsourcing, the better. It may be that the outsourcing supplier appointed will be able to provide interim resources on a consultancy basis, until the outsourcing contract is agreed.

Consultants

Consultants who have wider outsourcing experience may be appointed, to advise the customer's outsourcing project management team to whom outsourcing will be unfamiliar. If the customer organization lacks the competence to manage the selection process or if there are political reasons for not making an internal appointment, the consultants may assume an important and influential role.

Among the characteristics essential for consultants are suitable experience, demonstrable integrity and an established methodology for giving their advice. Client references should be followed up. The consultants should be genuinely independent, so that they can advise objectively on setting strategy and managing the bid process. There is therefore a very strong case for arguing that they should be free from any links with outsourcing companies. In any event, it is generally highly undesirable, although not unknown, for a consultancy firm to advise a customer in making the decision as to outsourcing, thereby acquiring in-depth knowledge of the customer's business, and then to succeed in getting the work either without any competition or by virtue of the advantages they will have gained over any other suppliers who enter the bid process later. The customer should beware of this situation.

Confidentiality

Before employing the services of specialist outsourcing consultants or issuing the invitation to tender, the customer must take the need for confidentiality into account. The knowledge that outsourcing is an option being considered might advisably be confined at the early stages to a very few people, both within the customer's organization and externally. The in-house IT staff may themselves not have learned of the situation. Moreover, in issuing the invitation to tender or in subsequent investigation by suppliers in order to produce their responses, the customer may have to make business information available which is not for general circulation.

The customer should therefore insist on a non-disclosure agreement being signed by any outsourcing consultants whose services are being used and, if appropriate, by any prospective suppliers. To be effective, this must be done in advance of any confidential information being made known to them.

A simple non-disclosure agreement for suppliers would state that, in consideration of the disclosure of all information in the invitation to tender about the proprietary, legal, business and technical matters of the customer and other information relating to it, the recipient of the information should use it only for the business purpose of making its response. The information should not be further disclosed, nor copied except as necessary, and should be furnished only to those of the supplier's employees who need to know it. For the supplier's benefit, there will be certain exceptions to what is regarded as confidential. These will include the disclosure of necessary information by the supplier to its accountants, legal advisers or any officials where there are legislative requirements. Information already known or within the public domain will also be excepted from confidentiality as will general concepts of information technology which would not be protectable. At the same time, the agreement can make it clear that the customer is not representing that there will inevitably be any further contracts in respect of the information, and that either party is at liberty to enter into similar agreements with other parties. The more coherently the requirements are set out, the easier the agreement will be to understand and enforce.

The supplier should agree not to disclose its customer's name in promotional materials or otherwise without consent. This provision may be overridden by the terms of the outsourcing contract once it becomes public knowledge, or it may be reinforced by the later agreement if it is a sensitive issue for the customer for any reason.

The invitation to tender and any other documents supplied should be clearly marked as confidential, for limited circulation and not to be copied, if these restrictions are appropriate. The message that the information has been supplied in confidence and subject to the non-disclosure agreement having been signed may be carried on the footer of each page. Copyright notices are not necessary, but may be helpful.

The customer may use a front-page disclaimer to emphasize that it is not committed to proceeding with outsourcing. This may state that the information is provided on the basis that: the document is an 'invitation to treat' and not a contractual offer; that any costs incurred by the supplier in preparing the response will be its own; that, although all efforts have been made to ensure that the information is correct, it is not warranted to be accurate or comprehensive; and that no undertaking is given that a supplier will be appointed resulting from any responses to the invitation to tender or otherwise.

In conjunction with this and as a matter of sensible practice, the customer should exercise care in what it does disclose. Although potential suppliers must have access to all information necessary for them to be able to make a reasonable bid, they should be able to see that the customer itself takes the need for confidentiality seriously. It is far easier to be pre-emptive than to have to react by invoking the agreement once damage has been done.

Conversely, in their tender responses, the tenderers will be disclosing commercially sensitive information about their charges, proposed methodologies and solutions and information about their own businesses. Thus their tender responses should be marked as confidential and not for copying, and for disclosure within the customer organization only to those individuals who need to know and to the customer's advisers.

The invitation to tender

In drawing up the invitation to tender, the customer should be conscious of the fact that the bid process can be extremely expensive for bidders, only one of whom is going to succeed.

Sufficient information must be provided to enable the potential suppliers to weigh up their experience in the light of the stated requirements and their ability to carry out the work profitably, so that they may realistically assess whether they actually want the contract.

The invitation to tender should address the objectives of outsourcing in context, defining the scope by identifying the services required. Suppliers should be asked to demonstrate generally:

- their understanding of the requirements
- how they intend to provide the services
- their proposed fees and charges
- their proposed management of the relationship.

For some areas, much detail will be available and any related performance criteria already known. Others will be sketchy. The focus should be on outputs, not methods, except where it is essential for certain organizational procedures to be followed. Links with other existing systems or services not part of the invitations to tender should be identified, along with any standards with which the supplier will be expected to conform.

A management synopsis may be asked for at the front of the response. It is also useful for the customer to have a summary of the contents.

Some ground rules may be laid down. The invitation to tender will delineate the criteria for selecting and evaluating the tenders. It should state that all contacts in connection with the tender should be made only through designated, named parties, whose names and addresses, telephone and fax numbers are given. This will be partly for confidentiality reasons, if the fact of going out to tender is not widely known within the customer organization. It will also be partly so that, if the suppliers have to spend time with the customer to find out more about its IT department's operation and resources in order to make their bids, this can be properly organized through one channel, giving all the suppliers equal opportunities and avoiding conflicts. A further reason is to ensure that the project manager keeps effective control of the bid process, by preventing bidders from trying to achieve results by side-stepping the agreed processes, by making overtures directly to senior directors, for example.

It may be categorically stated that the customer reserves the right to disqualify bidders who do not respond in the format requested. It will be far easier to compare responses which follow the same sequence. References should be requested and followed up.

An indicative timetable may be given, but a specific schedule will be an unnecessary commitment by the customer. It would be reasonable to state the timeframe within which presentations will be given from those bids which are shortlisted, and an anticipated date by which the selection of supplier will be made. Actual dates should be specified only if they are likely to be adhered to.

Tenderers will be given a deadline for responding to the invitation to tender; this should allow enough time for a thorough response to be given. Their response to the invitation to tender will be a document setting out the ways in which they believe they can meet the requirements and, in certain cases, they will also have the opportunity to make a presentation.

Criteria in choosing the supplier

Important elements in selecting a supplier are its financial viability and reliability. It is an essential prerequisite to an ongoing working relationship that supplier and customer should both feel comfortable about building a long-term co-operative relationship together. The following are basic questions for including in the invitation to tender, which the customer should expand as appropriate and which will need positive answers from the supplier.

- **Experience**
  - What is the supplier's company history and track record? How many years experience does the supplier have in outsourcing? Is it a new company or has this work developed logically from what it was doing before? Are outsourcing services part of the supplier's core business, or is more time spent in publishing or implementing software?
  - How many staff are there? Is there a structure to allow for career development, with different levels of experience and reporting relationships? Is there evidence of investment by the supplier in the resources needed to support the service?

    For how many clients are outsourcing services being provided? Are references willingly given? Are any clients similar to the potential customer in type of business, size, installation? Are any existing clients direct competitors of the customer? Would this cause a problem?
  - Does the supplier have experience of the customer's operating platforms, configurations and systems?
  - What is the size of the outsourcing company? Only a handful would be able to claim that they would be capable of handling certain public sector tenders or other large-scale outsourcings alone.
- **Quality**
  - What evidence is there of the skill, professional qualifications and experience of the supplier's staff?
  - What is the supplier's attitude to quality measurement and management?
  - Is there accreditation of Investors in People or ISO 9000?

- **Compatibility**
  - Will the supplier and customer have shared expectations in terms of cultural match, treatment of staff, codes of practice, shared vision of technology and style of management?
  - Is the business language similar? Are management attitudes consistent? This will be particularly significant if the customer's staff are to be transferred.
- **Staff**
  - What will be the career prospects, training opportunities, pension arrangements and benefits for transferred staff?
- **Flexibility**
  - Is the supplier independent of hardware manufacturers and software suppliers?
  - Will the supplier be able to support future business requirements in terms of expansion and change to the computer systems?
  - Is the supplier innovative? Will different strategies for better utilization of resources and assets be proposed?
- **Costs**
  Of course these are a major consideration, but not irrespective of other factors. It is crucial that comparisons between the potential suppliers are made on the same basis; that the costs are for similar services and cover equivalent matters, ascertaining that like is being compared with like. A basis is needed for evaluating variable costs – for example for future developments, enhancements and variations. Some suppliers use the British Computer Society Industry Structure Model to identify grades of staff to which charging rates can be applied. In order to compare proposals, the customer needs to create a model of variable services to be priced for each supplier.
- **Financial viability**
  - Is the outsourcing supplier a subsidiary company within a larger group? Who is the real owner of the company? If a risk is perceived in awarding a contract to a supplier who is a subsidiary, a guarantee or indemnity may be

required from the parent company, so that, if the subsidiary's business were to founder, the parent company would take over entire responsibility for the contract. Nevertheless, this should not be a substitute for properly evaluating the financial strength and capability of the supplier.

These requirements, tailored to the customer's needs, should be translated into representations which are confirmed as contractual acknowledgements by the supplier.

The draft contract

A draft contract or contract structure may be included with the invitation to tender. Tenderers should be asked to bid on these contract terms and to include in their tenders any proposed amendments to them.

The supplier's pricing will be based on its usual terms of business. Its costings for the response can allow for any differences in the terms as required by the customer.

Any proposals or modifications to the contract terms put forward by the tenderers should be assessed for their legal and commercial effects and compared with the tenor of the rest of the response. A supplier may claim to be flexible in providing services to meet varying requirements of the customer and yet object to a contract term permitting changes to the services.

Assessing the suppliers' responses

The customer's evaluation of the responses should be a rigorous process, in order to make reasoned comparisons among the tenderers. A list of selection criteria should be drawn up to ensure a consistent approach by each of the panel members concerned in making the evaluation. If one of the bids is from the in-house team, the technical part of the evaluation should be conducted by an independent professional, such as an external consultant.

A structured, disciplined evaluation process should be adopted for all but relatively minor selections. This must include predetermined criteria, devised from the customer's statement of requirements and graded according to relative importance both as to the overall topics and individual elements within each topic. Model responses may be constructed for each element on a scale of (for example) adequate to excellent, prepared independently of the contents of any proposal; by this means, proposals can be assessed objectively against a common model, rather than being compared with each other. The scoring should make provision for awarding marks on the quality of individual responses and also for the separate application of a confidence rating to significant elements. The latter may require a verification process, especially where innovative features appear in proposals.

Reference site visits should be used to produce confidence ratings for specific elements. The suppliers on the final shortlist may be invited to give a presentation in support of their bids. Preparing for, and attending, presentations is a time-consuming exercise both for suppliers and for customers, and only those few tenderers who are the final serious contenders should be asked to do so.

Supplier presentations should have a clearly defined purpose such as elucidation of proposals and verification, to be carried out at working level with the evaluation team (or its leaders). The presentations will thus be an opportunity to assess some of the statements made in the individual responses, to follow through those which need expanding, to weigh up the suitability of the approach of the potential suppliers in the context of the customer's culture, and to open up the discussion. The objective is to find the supplier best suited to working with the customer on a long-term basis. Information on what is going to be required at the presentations may be provided to the tenderers in advance.

The customer may ask for the presentation to be made by the members of the management team who it is proposed will be delivering the services, in order to meet them. Numbers should be limited. There is no advantage in the supplier bringing along everyone who will be having anything at all to do with the contract.

Confidence in the fairness of the selection procedure is important. Suppliers make large investments of resources, effort and costs in bidding. Records should be kept of the assessment of the responses to tender and the presentations. A debriefing for those bidders who failed is an essential exercise in the public sector to justify the choice that was made. It is also good practice for the private sector, in that it assists the unsuccessful suppliers to do better in the future.

Relationship of the parties

The outsourcing relationship must be kept at arm's length. Circumstances change. Nothing can be relied on to last in a commercial, industrial or public service environment. The parties negotiating the agreement will not necessarily be the same as the parties liaising over the life of the contract to carry out the services.

Suppliers use various terms both in discussions and their promotional literature to denote their ideal relationship with the customer: joint venture, joint sourcing, co-sourcing, partnering, partnership. Although the term 'partnership' is frequently encountered as representing cooperation, communication and commitment, its legal meaning carries specific connotations, being a relationship between two or more parties carrying on a business together with a view to making a profit. The profits – or, conversely, the losses – are shared between the parties according to what they agree or in proportion to their capital contribution. Thus, business partners are also responsible for each other's debts and other obligations. Partners are agents of the partnership. Any one partner has the power to bind the other partners in relation to obligations incurred to third parties in partnership matters. This is *not* what an outsourcing relationship is normally about.

Moreover, a partnership is one kind of 'fiduciary relationship', which implies more onerous responsibilities for partners than those which apply in a normal contractual relationship. It arises where there is a special relationship between the parties concerned, often where one party is in a stronger position than the other, such as employee and employer, or guardian and ward. It is a relationship of trust or confidentiality, legally implying obligations of 'good faith' – honesty, openness and good intentions.

The outsourcing relationship is not therefore a genuine legal partnership, and it is not a term which should be recklessly bandied about by suppliers in their promotional materials and marketing presentations, or used in the contract. The profits of each party derive from different activities. The supplier's profits are the result of providing outsourcing services, and perhaps other sorts of information systems services, to numbers of organizations. If the customer is a profit-making business, its profits will arise from its core business, whether this is selling goods or supplying services. The customer may be a different kind of organization, such as a public sector authority providing a service, but not for profit. If the services supplied are unsatisfactory, the customer has the ultimate right to terminate the contract or not to renew it.

IT 'partnerships' in commercial projects will be, at most, a form of joint venture, consortium or partnering agreement, rather than a legally defined partnership.

As one head of computer management services said:

> If you derive a lot of competitive advantage from IT you are unlikely to outsource or develop a strategic alliance, and if you just use IT to cut costs, then it's like outsourcing the office cleaning, in which case why have a strategic partnership with the FM company?[2]

A commercial joint venture is a relationship in which a business is formed for a deliberate purpose between two or more parties who each take a share. For example, if a company has a problem of overcapacity on its mainframe, an outsourcing company may be set up resulting from a management buy-out by a customer's former IT managers, or as a joint venture between an outsourcing supplier and the IT department of an organization, primarily in order to supply IT services to that organization, but with the ultimate aim of extending its supply of services to other companies. The customer may contribute market and application knowledge for future commercial activities while the supplier's contribution will be in terms of technical skills and commercial awareness. The supplier will be in a position to make more extensive use of the computer facilities or to sell the additional capacity, and the customer and supplier will each benefit.

Both parties to a joint venture need to be committed to its success, and neither party can easily withdraw from the relationship at an early stage without suffering financially or commercially. There will be additional administrative, legal, audit and management responsibilities to take into account and, without a proper development strategy, the effort involved may not be justifiable.

If the reasons for considering a joint venture vehicle are to develop particular vertical services but the customer has no real interest in long-term involvement in its management, the customer could make a financial investment in the supplier in the manner of a venture capitalist in return for a participating preferential dividend for some years with a guaranteed buy-out (at a multiple of profits) at some future point.

If the customer is considering a joint venture in order to benefit from a share of profits obtained from exploiting its transferred assets, a profit-sharing obligation in the outsourcing agreement may be just as effective.

However, these variants are relatively exceptional. The normal outsourcing contract should state unequivocally that the parties are independent of each other. If the supplier is being granted any authority to negotiate licences and hardware contracts or any other terms and conditions on the customer's behalf, this should be stated, and it should be made clear whether the supplier does so in its own name or the customer's, so that this authority is not extended to any other contracts for which it is not intended by the customer.

'Partnering' is a current expression for some contracts. It originates in the construction industry, from where this definition derives:

> Partnering is a management approach used by two or more organisations to achieve specific business objectives by maximising the effectiveness of each participant's resources. The approach is based on mutual objectives, an agreed method of problem resolution and an active search for continuous measurable improvements.[3]

This implies teamwork in performing the contract and a commitment to making it work, yet without the wholesale commitment of partnership.

A partnering contract may reduce confrontation, but it does carry a risk that the relationship will be too close, removing any scope for competition or innovation.

The supplier may incidentally be in a position of considerable power in awarding contracts to third parties as part of the outsourcing. In its own interests, the customer may wish to spell out in the contract the boundaries of propriety: that the supplier should take no commission, bribe or other financial incentive where it is negotiating third-party contracts on behalf of its customer, whether hardware, software or services, and should ensure that all its staff are fully aware of this. One stage less exacting than this which may be acceptable to the customer is that if the supplier is permitted to take commission, it should disclose it openly in advance.

The right choice of supplier for the particular outsourcing requirements is paramount to the success of the relationship.

Notes

1 Jason Hobby, 'Out But in Control', *VAR Journal*, March 1996.
2 John Watson, Head of Computer Management Services at British Nuclear Fuels, quoted in *Computer Weekly*, May 1993.
3 Professor John Bennett and Sarah Jayes (1995), *Trusting the Team – The Best Practice Guide to Partnering in Construction*, Reading: University of Reading Centre for Strategic Studies in Construction.

4 Public procurement

In the UK, as in the rest of the European Union (EU), the civil service, local authorities and other public sector organizations are regulated at law in their procurement practice. The rules and procedures concerned with the procurement of services, including outsourcing services, in the UK public sector are known as the 'public procurement regime'. Utilities – that is, companies in the water, energy, transport and telecommunications sectors – are also regulated according to similar, although not identical, procedures which also form part of the procurement regime, whether or not they are in the public sector.

The regime operates by means of EC Procurement Directives which apply to contracts in the public and utility sectors throughout member states in the EU and also to those states which are now part of the European Free Trade Association (EFTA) – Norway, Iceland and Liechtenstein. Contracting authorities and utilities must award contracts according to objective criteria, following the procedures. In the UK, the legislation is implemented by means of statutory instruments.

The full regime applies to public works, public supplies and public services. However, this chapter outlines the basic elements of the public procurement regime applying to services and thus to IT outsourcing services.

Customers affected by the regime are bound to be familiar with the legal requirements. The legislation is complicated, and specialist legal advice is strongly recommended for suppliers interested in participating, since they will need to be acquainted with the details.

The legal framework

The UK Regulations implementing the Directives which are the basis of the public procurement regime are the Public Services Contracts Regulations 1993,[1] which implement the EC Services Directive.[2] They cover the award of contracts to service-providers for all the white-collar and professional services in the public sector to which the regime applies.

Contracts for services awarded by utilities are subject to a separate Directive, the Consolidated Utilities Directive,[3] implemented in the UK by the Utilities Contracts Regulations.[4]

The importance of public procurement

The general principle fundamental to the EU is that it should comprise a single internal market for trading in goods and services. This implies that any business within the EU, in whatever country it is based, should be able to bid for work anywhere else in the EU. When looking at whether this precept works successfully in practice, the public sector is of particular concern because throughout the EU, it comprises an enormous market for supply and service contracts – about 15–20 per cent of the overall gross domestic product (GDP).

Nevertheless, national products and services have always tended to be favoured when public money is being spent. On average, fewer than 2 per cent of contracts in the public sector are awarded outside a national territory, in contrast to the normal figure for imports which is more in the order of 20 per cent. These national markets in the public sector are a major hurdle in preventing the achievement of a genuine internal market in the EU member states. The belief is that the effects of competition in the commercial marketplace will ultimately bring savings to taxpayers.

The purpose of the public procurement regime

The objective of the public procurement regime is to ensure that all public contracts over a given value are publicized and awarded according to principles of transparency, non-discrimination and competition. This means that the specification of the features demanded must list genuine requirements, there must be open competition and there should be no unfair discrimination in the selection of suppliers. At the same time there are procedures available which offer certain limited remedies at law to suppliers who believe that they have been maltreated, and which provide for legal sanctions against customers where there has been a failure to comply with the rules.

By means of the procurement procedures, public sector and utility bodies can identify a range of contractors in their search for the best value, whether the contractors are based in the UK or elsewhere in the EU.

The benefits for suppliers lie in the potential for securing new and increased business opportunities which they would not otherwise necessarily have known about, not only in the UK but across the member states, by open competition on equal terms within the public sector. At the same time, however, they need to reinforce their position in their home market, where they may themselves be subject to greater competition.

Who has to follow the rules?

'Contracting authorities', having contracts to award for the provision of services, include central and local government and other bodies governed by public law, including various quasi-public entities, such as urban development corporations, fire authorities, police authorities and national health services.

'Utilities' cover almost all the water, energy, transport and telecommunications industries – including the privatized water and power generating companies, gas, electricity and oil industries, airport and port authorities, the rail transport operators, operating either as public authorities or undertakings or on the basis of special or exclusive rights granted under authority of the state. Bus transport is excluded if other operators are able to provide services in the same area under equivalent conditions.

Types of contract

All types of commercial contracts for services awarded by a contracting authority or a utility are subject to the procurement rules unless they are specifically excepted or the value of the contract falls below financial thresholds which vary according to the type of contract. If the contracts are for works or supplies rather than for services, they will fall to be dealt with under the other parts of the procurement regime as appropriate, so that overlap is avoided and so that no contract is subject to more than one set of Regulations. If a contract is for both goods and services, the value of each part must be calculated and, if the value for the services exceeds the value of the goods, the contract will be defined as a services contract.

Exceptions include employment contracts and agreements for arbitration and conciliation services, which do not need to be advertised across the EU. Contracts for IT services, however, do come within the procurement rules.

There are two levels of public service contracts, identified as 'Part A' and 'Part B'; these are the headings under which the different types of contracts are listed in the Public Services Regulations, according to the functional area of the services. The rules apply in full to 'Part A' services which include contracts for 'computer and related services'. 'Part B' services, such as legal, education, or health and social services, are subject only to certain of the rules.

Threshold values

The Regulations apply only if the value of a services procurement contract will equal or exceed value thresholds. These are intended to confine the number of contracts which are subject to the regime to a number which can be properly monitored and effectively implemented. The values differ according to the type of procurement. They are expressed in ECUs and are updated at two-yearly intervals in equivalent values in the national currencies within the EU. They are fixed for two years in advance in each currency regardless of the ECU's fluctuations against European currencies and regardless of sterling's fluctuations against other European currencies. Authorities therefore have no reason to delay decisions on contracts during times of uncertainty.

Generally speaking, the estimated value is the price to be paid for the contract, exclusive of VAT. The calculation for the estimated value of an outsourcing contract may be difficult. Where a total price cannot be specified, there are detailed provisions for assessing the value. Rules are laid down to ensure that a single large contract cannot be separated into units so that, in isolation, each individual contract would be below the limit and thereby avoid the rules. Each contract must be examined to see if it is in fact one of a series.

Thus, if a number of contracts are awarded at the same time for a single requirement for services, the estimated value of each single contract is counted towards the aggregated value of all of them. Where contracts for particular types of service are regular or renewed, the aggregate value of similar contracts for the same types of service over the previous year adjusted to take account of anticipated changes in quality and costs for the forthcoming year, or the value estimated for the next 12 months or for the whole contract duration, has to be taken into account in order to calculate the threshold. The deemed value of a contract under which services are to be provided to a contracting authority for a fixed period of longer than four years, or indefinitely, is obtained by multiplying the monthly value by 48 – whatever the actual duration of the contract. Where there is an option to terminate the contract after a certain time, the highest amount payable is taken as the value of the contract.

General procedure and notices

In general, under the public procurement regime, contracting authorities must:

* follow specified procedures in seeking offers
* give notices about the contract in prescribed formats at various stages of the procedures
* give fair consideration to bidders from anywhere in the EU
* award the contract according to specified criteria
* publish details of the award made

The rules for utilities are less stringent and prescriptive than for contracting authorities.

All public notices required in connection with the tendering and award processes by public authorities or utilities where the value exceeds the threshold must be publicized in the *Official Journal of the European Union*, (*Official Journal*). Notices stating the changes made every two years to the thresholds are also published in it. The *Official Journal* comes in three sections: C – which publishes notices such as the one relating to the threshold value; L – which publishes Community legislation; and S – which publishes contract details in the form of notices.

The S-series is also available online as the *Tenders Electronic Daily*, referred to as *TED*. It is more selective than the *Official Journal* and is therefore easier to read. The addresses for the *Official Journal* and *TED* are given at the end of this book.

The EC Office for Official Publications in Luxembourg ensures that the notices are published within 12 days of receipt. They must try to publish within five days if requested to do so by electronic mail, telex or fax, where reduced time limits are sought for reasons of urgency. Thus the information is accessible by subscription to the publication or to the database.

These advertisements are a means of making sure that any company who might have an interest in bidding can discover that there is the opportunity of work.

Some companies specialize in scanning the *Official Journal* to select notices of potential bidding opportunities which will be of interest to their clients.

The procedure for contracting authorities requires three kinds of notices at various stages: the prior information notice, the contract notice and the award notice. There are model forms of notices which should be followed, each containing specified information.

Prior information notices are published soon after the start of a contracting authority's financial year, for the purposes of announcing those services contracts which fall within the regime which it expects to be awarding in that year.

The equivalent notice for utilities is the *periodic indicative notice*. This is advance information to contractors who might be interested, and avoids any obligation for the utility to publish a new notice for every individual contract during those 12 months. It can indicate that the restricted or negotiated procedure will apply to a proposed contract and request those interested to write and say so.

Once a decision is taken to proceed, a *contract notice* gives more information about an individual contract, according to which specific procedure is being followed – inviting tenders (the open procedure) or requesting interested parties to participate (the restricted or the negotiated procedure). Under the negotiated procedure, the notice may be dispensed with in certain circumstances.

The *award notice* is published when the contract has been awarded.

Tendering

In inviting tenders and negotiating for the award of individual contracts, the contracting authority must follow one of the three defined procedures: open, restricted or negotiated.

In general, either the open or restricted procedure must be followed. The negotiated procedure should be used only exceptionally. The tendering procedure can be avoided altogether only in narrowly defined restricted circumstances, such as extreme urgency. There are time limits specified throughout the procedures, consisting in every case of a set number of days during which notices must be published, information supplied and tenders received, in order to provide proper opportunities to interested parties.

Utilities have more leeway in the system than do the contracting authorities. The rationale for this is that they were already expected to operate commercially and cost-effectively, and that they were therefore less biased in favour of national suppliers. The rules have the same basis but allow some adaptability. There are higher threshold values, and the utilities do not have to comply with such detailed rules on checking the financial and technical suitability of tenderers.

They have a free choice of which of the three procedures to follow, once an invitation to tender – a 'call for competition' – has been made. Thus they are given wider discretion to use the negotiated procedure, avoiding the need for formal tenders. They may establish their own criteria for selecting participants provided that they are objective. They may operate qualification systems with objective criteria and rules, in order to establish preselected lists of suitable suppliers for negotiating for particular kinds of service without further advertising. They can agree the time limits which should apply.

Open, restricted and negotiated procedures

Under the *open procedure*, no preselection takes place. The invitation is open to all interested parties to submit priced bids.

The authority must consider all the tenders received and select according to the permitted criteria. This is rarely used for IT services.

In the restricted procedure, and in the negotiated procedure preceded by an advertised call for competition, contracting authorities select from suppliers who have responded to a prior information notice, suppliers who have replied to a contract notice or suppliers who are qualified under the rules of the qualification system. The selection must be on the defined objective criteria.

Under the *restricted procedure*, the authority selects certain suppliers to submit tenders out of those who have initially expressed interest in the contract advertised. This permits an early screening process on the basis of such criteria as technical ability and financial standing and will limit the number of suppliers from amongst whom the final decision must be made. Enough contractors should pass this first selection stage 'to ensure genuine competition'. If the authority decides to set a limit on the numbers, it should be between five and 20 – provided that at least these numbers have responded.

Written invitations to tender must be sent out simultaneously to each of these selected suppliers. Rules defined in the Regulations detail what documentation goes with the invitation, whether it has to be enclosed with the invitation or whether it can be obtained from a stated address. The short-listed supplier candidates will be invited to interview or to give presentations to the evaluation panel.

Post-tender negotiation is not permitted except to clarify or supplement the tenders put forward. The successful contractor will be announced, and unsuccessful tenderers must be given an explanation of the decision in relation to them, on request.

In either the open or restricted procedure, a tenderer may ask for clarification of the invitation to tender and the information provided with it. All tenderers will be circulated with the replies to ensure that the same information is available to all.

The *negotiated procedure* avoids the time-consuming general competition of the open and restricted procedures and therefore offers advantages if it can be complied with. Like the restricted procedure, it is a two-stage process. A contract notice of the intention to seek offers for a public services contract must still be published in the *Official Journal*. A decision is made after consulting with contractors of the utility or contracting authority's choice and considering the results of the consultation.

The negotiated procedure is more relaxed than the other two procedures and is the most limited in application. However, in practice it is used extensively, although a contracting authority has to be able to justify this choice of procedure. The justification may be because: tenders received under open or restricted procedures were irregular or unacceptable, or none was received; or because the nature of the contract does not allow prior pricing or a precise specification (this is often the reason the negotiated procedure is followed); or because the contract is for research and development. The negotiated procedure may also sometimes be used without publishing a contract notice – for example, in the absence of appropriate tenders in response to an open or restricted procedure; or where for technical, artistic or legal reasons, the contract may only be carried out by a particular contractor.

The advertisement need give only enough information to attract appropriate bidders. The tender documentation will include the detailed specification, which may be refined during the initial period.

Technical specifications

There are also rules set out in the Directives on setting technical specifications and standards as a requirement for the services to be supplied and the goods and materials associated with the services.

The broad reasoning behind this is that the existence of various technical specifications and different national standards stands in the way of the free movement of goods and services within the European Union. Another main factor intrinsic to IT is to encourage exchange of information, open systems and systems interoperability. Purchasers should not be unnecessarily tied in to suppliers if they are upgrading or enhancing their systems. Contracting authorities must not set standards – such as those which are currently promulgated only in the authority's country – which could exclude otherwise valid competition.

Standards should be specified as a requirement only when it is reasonable to do so. Any requirement for standards must be stated in the contract documents sent out to tenderers. If there are any relevant European standards they should be the first point of reference. However, often there are none which would be applicable or those which exist may be incompatible with existing equipment, would cause excessive cost or would limit innovation. In any of these cases, other technical standards may be specified, including any British standards.

Selecting the supplier

The suitability of the tenderer must be assessed in terms of soundness and integrity, economic and financial standing, and technical capability. Additional criteria may be specified provided that they are not discriminatory. The only grounds for disqualification of tenderers are where they fall short of the economic, financial or technical standards required. Thus, grounds for disqualification by contracting authorities which are non-discriminatory and therefore permitted include, not surprisingly, the supplier's insolvency or gross misconduct, its reputation, professional qualifications, economic standing and technical knowledge and ability.

The only grounds on which to award a public services contract are either that the tender is the most economically advantageous to the authority or that it is the lowest-priced. These are not necessarily the same. The former criterion allows factors other than price to be considered, such as 'value for money', quality and technical merit. These factors have to be listed, ideally in priority sequence, in the notice to prospective tenderers or supplied as part of the documentation. Factors which are not listed may not be taken into account. A tender which is the lowest price but abnormally low for the transaction concerned may be rejected, although an explanation should be sought before it is disqualified. A report that this has occurred has to be sent to the European Commission.

A contract award notice will be published in the *Official Journal* once the award has been made. A supplier is entitled to be informed, within 15 days of its request, of reasons for its rejection. Unsuccessful suppliers will have invested time and money in bidding and are entitled to be given the reasons why they were unsuccessful, so that they can see that the process has been fair. Contractors should find this helpful for their future tender strategy, but they may also review the reasons given to consider whether there is any legal redress.

The statistics show that not all awards are yet notified to the *Official Journal* as they should be.

Complaints about awards

EC Directives, setting out procedures for lodging a complaint against contracting authorities or utilities,[5] and detailing the remedies available if the procedures are not followed, have been implemented into UK law.

Unsuccessful tenderers based in the EU, who have genuine cause for complaint over the selection procedures, have remedies through the courts directly against contracting authorities and utilities who do not comply with the public procurement obligations. For example, a supplier may believe it would have won the procurement process had it been properly conducted, or may believe it was unfairly excluded from bidding.

If the contract at issue has not yet been awarded, but a supplier believes that its own rights are about to be infringed, and it can move fast, it can apply for an injunction to suspend an unlawful tender procedure, set aside an unlawful decision or stop an award from being made. This injunction is an interim remedy granted before the full case is heard. A risk for the supplier who brings these types of proceedings is that if it loses the case, it could end up having to compensate the authority. The supplier may have to give an undertaking itself that it will pay any damages which the contracting authority suffers through the injunction, perhaps on account of delay in being able to implement the contract award.

Damages can be awarded against a contracting authority that fails to comply with the procurement regime. If the contract has been awarded, an aggrieved supplier which believes that it has suffered loss as a result of a breach of the procurement rules – in practice because it has not won a contract that it believes it should have – and which can quantify the loss it consequently suffers may claim damages against the contracting authority concerned through the courts, if the procedure was not complied with or the contract has been unfairly awarded to another party. There is no guidance in the Regulations on the level of damages. The court must assess whether the supplier would have been awarded the contract had the proper procedures been followed, and this would form the basis for damages, expressed as potential loss of profit. The only direct loss might be confined to the cost of tendering, any further loss being too speculative. For a supplier which was unable to tender because it did not know about the contract, the damages would be even more difficult to assess.

An action must be brought promptly and, in any event, within three months of the date the grounds first arose, unless the court extends that time limit by reason of exceptional circumstances.

The European Commission is itself entitled to take action to enforce the Directives within member states, and a supplier may alternatively make a complaint to this body. While this is confidential and avoids legal costs, it is not a means by which the supplier can obtain damages, since the Commission brings actions against member states rather than the defaulting contracting authority. Since contract awards are not overturned once the contract has been entered into, involving the Commission would give no practical remedy to a disgruntled supplier.

Effectiveness of the public procurement regime

More information about the contract plans of contracting authorities has become available as a result of the regime, although, from their point of view, correctly following the procedures entails a great deal of paperwork.

One view is that more efforts should be directed towards enforcing the regime. Abuses may arise from using irrelevant criteria or from overuse of the accelerated or negotiated tendering procedure. The provisions for enforcement and for obtaining legal remedies are little used. Most companies will be reluctant to jeopardize their future business with a contracting authority by taking legal proceedings. They may fear that somehow they may not be selected in future for that authority, or indeed for others. It is difficult to prove damage, and the sums awarded may not be felt to be worth the effort of bringing proceedings. Moreover a complainant has to act swiftly – within three months of the award. These are the issues which may underlie the small amount of litigation and the few complaints so far.

Alternatively, of course, it could mean that the procedures are being properly followed.

Conclusion

The intention of the public procurement regime is to encourage new opportunities for competition in order to bring ultimate cost savings to public authorities and utilities. The legal requirements and basic contract terms must be considered at the outset of outsourcing.

However, as the rules and regulations are drawn up to apply generally, to different situations, different services and for different legal systems, they are complicated and are perceived as bureaucratic.

Involvement in the selection process can be expensive, both for customers who have to prepare documentation and weigh up the merits of different tenderers and for tenderers who have to respond to enquiries and submit proposals, many of which need to be fairly comprehensive.

In practice there is a perception that the public procurement regime does not operate as effectively as intended to achieve its objective of an open market. The rules are not applied, interpreted or enforced consistently throughout the EU. It remains unusual for businesses to bid for contracts abroad, or for foreign businesses to bid for work in the UK.

Both the European Commission and the UK government are keeping the operation of competition and fairness in public sector procurement under review.

Notes

1 Public Services Contracts Regulations 1993 (SI 1993 No. 3228).
2 EC Services Directive (92/50/EEC).
3 93/38/EEC – Coordinating Procedures of Entities Operating in Excluded Sectors (water, energy, transport and telecommunications) (OJ1993L 99/84).
4 Utilities Contracts Regulations 1996 (SI19960/2911).
5 The Compliance Directive (89/665/EEC) and the Utilities Remedies Directive (92/13/EEC).

5 Services and service level agreements

An outsourcing contract is defined by reference to the services which are being contracted out. The customer is paying for the provision of services by the supplier according to agreed standards – the service levels. The ongoing assessment of the success of the contract will be by the process of overseeing and reviewing the standards of service which are achieved in practice. Rebates or payments may be made by the supplier to the customer in the event of failure of services to achieve key service levels.

One of the most important parts of the contract will therefore concern the services and service levels. The supplier will give a commitment to provide the specified services and, associated with this obligation, will be a further undertaking to provide the services according to the service levels.

The services and the service levels required will be unique to the customer organization. Although the services being outsourced by two different organizations may be apparently similar, the substantive details, relative priorities and performance criteria for one company may well be irrelevant for the other. Moreover, over time and with experience in working with them, it is highly probable that the services and service levels initially agreed will change. The opportunity for revision should be built into the contract.

Services

The services to be provided should be described in the contract, in terms of their scope, the extent of the supplier's management responsibilities in relation to them and how much flexibility is to be allowed for in the case of any additional services required. The customer may be able to include a sweep-up clause for other services not specifically defined, which will be useful in ensuring that everything can come under the outsourcing umbrella. However, a supplier should beware of generic open-ended statements of its service obligations over and above the services which have been originally listed.

The first general statements identifying the services should set out the primary obligations of the supplier: what the services are for; whether this is a statement about management of operational data processing, networks or help desks; for selective outsourcing; or a general statement that the services comprise the whole IT capability. The committed time within which the services are to be provided should be clear: is it to be round the clock, every day of the year, or some lesser availability? The location of the processing or the destination of the outputs may need to be mentioned. The supplier may be undertaking to run efficient systems for tracking and managing problems and changes, to coordinate operations and procedures with the customer, end users, and other suppliers or generally to comply with service levels. Capacity planning, security management, training and quality control may also be considered as part of the services provided by the supplier. Resilience – core facilities, degraded service, recovery and so on – must be addressed. These or other responsibilities may be allocated between the supplier and customer. Who is to ensure that documentation is up-to-date and who controls its circulation? Will the supplier want to exclude responsibility for data preparation or for faults on input made by the customer or by a third party? Who is in charge of job control and scheduling? Who controls the maintenance and renewal of equipment at the customer's or end user's premises?

These are the sort of initial questions which may need to be asked.

- How are the services defined? For example:
  - Business area: purchasing, finance, production
  - Type of service: operations, development, admin- istration, management, mainten- ance and support, security
  - System: order processing, credit control
  - Operation: online, batch processing, main- frame, distributed.
- For the scope of the services, are the following relevant for each particular service?

Service hours

- Will the services all be carried out during normal working hours (which should be defined)?
- Is there to be provision for extending normal working hours on notice?
- Are public holidays, weekends and overtime ever to be allowed for, as a matter of course, or only if the customer gives advance notice (and how much notice)?
- Are certain times and availabilities more important than others – for example, tax year end, daily close of business?
- Are there strict deadlines?
- How will emergencies be catered for?
- Do the timescales depend on the inputs being received by a certain time?

Volumes and capacities

- What are the average, typical and maximum volumes?
- What is the anticipated growth?

- What is the actual and target availability?
- Will any of the service levels depend on external lines of supply? If so, the commitment must be backed up in the contracts with the third parties concerned.

Exclusions

- What is to be allowed for as scheduled unavailability – for equipment maintenance, implementation of new software, installation of new equipment, building servicing, staff training, for example? Can this be carried out during normal working hours or will the customer pay the extra costs of overtime?

Maintenance and support

- What is the level of preventive and remedial maintenance to be provided?
- Who is responsible for supplying and maintaining peripherals and operational consumables, such as magnetic tapes, discs and cartridges?
- What are the anticipated recovery times for unscheduled service outages?

Help desk

- What response times are expected for the initial response to queries and problems?
- Will they be categorized by priority?
- How long should it take to solve a problem?
- Is there an escalation procedure for increasing resources or for a commitment to finding a solution?

System development services

- Can performance requirements be identified at this stage for business analysis, feasibility studies, package selection, specification and design?

- How far is the supplier expected to take the initiative in identifying business opportunities for new technology or systems?

Education and training

- What are the proposals for training new end users and the supplier's new employees?

Quality assurance and engineering standards

- What inspection, testing requirements, and sign-off procedures will be required (for the system development life cycle in particular)?
- Is there to be formal quality control and quality assurance – for example, compliance with a standard such as ISO 9000 or BS 7799? Is information security management to be part of the service? (The standards themselves will not be a substitute for working out the service levels appropriate to the installation.)
- Are codes of conduct or codes of practice for staff to be included?

Back-up arrangements

- Are there adequate contingency planning and disaster recovery procedures?

Defining the service levels

Service levels demonstrate the performance of 'reasonable skill and care' and are the key to a successful outsourcing relationship. They are the specification of mutually acceptable, measurable standards of performance by the supplier, which are agreed to be reasonably attainable in practice under normal circumstances. They should not be mere hoped-for, optimistic targets.

Some provisions will be implied at law into a contract, whether or not they are actually expressly worded. Under legislation covering the supply of services, it is implicit in all services contracts that the services will be carried out with reasonable skill and care within a reasonable time.[1] As the definition of 'reasonable' depends on the circumstances, it is therefore more practical for both parties that the supplier give precise commitments about skill, care and timeframes.

As part of the process of compiling the service levels, decisions need to be made on how much time and energy should be devoted to measuring them.

The emphasis in drawing up the service levels should be on deliverables, not processes – on ends, not means. In principle, the customer should not be concerned with the methods of delivery. For example, it may not matter to the customer how often a process has to be run to produce a result, if the service-level target of a report produced within a time limit is met. In some cases, particular procedures may need to be followed – for example, to ensure compatibility between two systems, or to satisfy the requirements of particular end users, or where they are directly related to the method of charging – but this should be regarded as an exception. It is normally the supplier's responsibility to decide how the objectives in the outsourcing are to be reached. If the customer stresses certain procedures or techniques, this could hamper an innovative supplier from finding different and more efficient routes to achieving the objectives.

All key services must be measurable. Some activities will be required as part of the services without operational damage actually resulting if they are not met. A supplier may claim to have high standards of courtesy, but levels of politeness are a subjective matter and not easily measurable in terms which both parties would be happy to accept. It may be a service requirement for the supplier's staff to dress appropriately, but it would not bring a system crashing down if a failure occurred, even if the existence of the failure could be agreed. There may be exceptions to this – perhaps for staff who meet the public as part of their work.

'Customer satisfaction' always provides scope for dispute. It may be important, particularly if the supplier makes promotional claims of its abilities in this area. If necessary, acceptable criteria must be agreed by both sides, but will probably be subjective and not readily amenable to enforcement by means of the normal incentives to performance discussed below. A solution may be to devise questionnaires for end users, offering responses in the form of numerical values to cover timeliness of information provided, quality of service, value for money and staff attitudes. Shortcomings which arise may have to be dealt with through management procedures.

A bland, generally worded undertaking to keep 'supplying the service previously supplied' is unlikely to be acceptable, although this principle may be a good starting-point (but not necessarily, if the main reason for outsourcing is to improve the service).

A commitment by the supplier to guarantee '98 per cent availability' is equally unsatisfactory, since it is open to various interpretations. What is the 'availability' to cover, and what does '98 per cent' mean? Is it actually a service where anything less than 100 per cent cannot be tolerated? For example, one breach of security may be one too many. Or, as is more likely, is a graduated failure pattern to be measured? There may be a general level of acceptability for a daily report to be produced within an agreed number of hours, and failures to an agreed level could accumulate to the point at which they are unacceptable over the defined period. Some of the services will be important only at particular times. Are there points at which failure is critical – say, for the month-end run or at end-of-year?

Thus measurement should be accurately defined and realistic. Can it be related to existing meaningful time parameters, the periods between meetings or accounting periods? Should this be consistently 98 per cent during working hours, and within a month? Further precision is necessary. Is it to be a calendar month or a rolling four-week period?

A service period may be measured as a precise band of time – such as a number of consecutive weeks, starting at 6 am on the first Monday where processing is continuous. The services can then be measured in terms of availability, response times, number of faults, time to repair and so on. Measurement may be by sampling. Where there are levels which fluctuate, should the best or the worst examples be taken?

The supplier must be able to meet the service level requirements if resources are temporarily inadequate because of holidays, illness, resignations, breakdowns or external failures.

In some cases service levels will be dependent on actions taken by the customer or third parties. This must be specified – for example, 'subject to the input data being received by noon on Day One, the report will be available by 9 am on Day Two'.

Charges are often explicitly linked to service level performance. In any case there is a direct relationship between the cost of the outsourcing contract and the levels of service which are acceptable. The ideal for the customer is error-free performance 100 per cent of the time. However, the cost of supplying this service overall, even if it were practically attainable, will normally be out of the question, although there may be specific exceptions for certain elements. The service levels represent what the customer is prepared to afford. The higher the level of service required, the less the margin of error which will be acceptable, and the more expensive the outsourcing will be.

It is important for both sides that the supplier recognize the quality of service expected by the customer. It is up to both parties to assess what is realistic, balancing cost against quality. The customer must decide what it will pay. The supplier must be satisfied that the service can be delivered profitably.

Existing service level measurements

Some customer organizations will already be measuring the services provided by the existing IT department. If they have critical manufacturing processes for which precision is required, for example, they may have quality assurance throughout the organization. In this event, the basic information will already be available for drawing up the service level agreements, and the task will be more easily manageable and take less time than having to start from scratch.

Indeed, one good way of preparing early for the prospect of outsourcing is for the customer to take the initiative in drawing up service levels well before the invitation to tender is issued. This in itself has been known, on the one hand, to improve responsiveness to end users by the IT department and, on the other, to create new expectations by the end users of what is sensibly achievable. Thus by enabling greater understanding of the role and functions of the IT department it may even help to ameliorate a political situation within an organization. It will also furnish a benchmark for comparison of what the IT department can offer as against external tenders. A possible side-effect would be to obviate the need for outsourcing!

If the supplier has to take the customer's existing figures, it will need to analyse the service level metrics and their history itself. Is there a record of consistency? The supplier needs to know whether the service levels have consistently been achieved and that the figures have been used in management control, over the period prior to the negotiations, normally at least the previous 12 months prior to contract signature.

The customer may be asked to warrant the service levels if the supplier has no means of independently checking their accuracy. This is not a meaningful warranty and should be resisted. How could it be disproved?

The supplier may be able to suggest improvements to any existing service levels. This will set the scene for a more cost-effective outsourcing relationship for the customer.

Agreeing the service levels

If there are no existing measures, or if current services are not meeting expectations, time will need to be spent by both parties in determining the service levels, ideally before the contract is signed. In reality, this may be an unattainable counsel of perfection. For various reasons, the initial exercise of producing the service level agreements will not always be completed by the time the outsourcing contract comes into effect.

Defining the service levels could be undertaken as a joint exercise, or the supplier may use its own experience in outsourcing and build on the knowledge it has gained in making its tender by carrying out the exercise itself. It may seek to impose a charge for this work.

If it is necessary to go ahead with the outsourcing before the service levels have been defined to both parties' satisfaction, temporary arrangements could be made at the start of the outsourcing – perhaps based on average performance levels currently being achieved in the business – and the requirements finalized during a transitional period after the contract has been signed and the outsourcing process introduced, and during which the services will be measured in order to set sustainable service levels before a given deadline or cutover point.

Where any service levels are stated 'to be agreed', this must be followed up at the project review meetings and noted; target dates for finalizing them should also be set. 'Agreements to agree' are not definite enough to be legally enforceable, but will state the common intention in an area where it is in the interests of both parties to have the service levels clarified eventually. This is not a procedure to be recommended, but sometimes there is no other way. It should not be considered as either a typical or satisfactory way of short-circuiting the negotiating process in order to get the contract signed. If possible, a procedure should be prescribed for agreeing the limits of the service levels with a fixed timetable and with resort to a special form of dispute resolution which should be laid down in the contract, to be invoked for any difficulties which arise in connection with the definition of service levels during this transitional period.

In whatever ways the exercise in setting service levels is carried out, both the supplier and the user must approve the results.

There should be some scope for flexibility. It will not automatically be possible to define all the service levels correctly at once, or to guarantee that they will remain the same should the business context and technology change. Furthermore, the risk of the slow decline of service levels during the contract term should be recognized.

The services themselves and their service levels should therefore be reviewed regularly to evaluate their continuing benefit. The supplier may be expected to provide additional or revised services if so required by the customer, subject to agreeing any further charges to be imposed, as part of the scope for varying the contract. New service levels may have to be agreed. The structure for meetings and the reports produced should facilitate the discussions and enable implementation of any updates or changes, under the variation procedures discussed in Chapter 11.

Respective roles in performance assessment

During the outsourcing, the supplier will be responsible for keeping the performance statistics. Automated processes will help maintain the statistics. Computer systems and software and other equipment, such as telecommunications equipment and network monitors, can provide much information as to usage and performance. This information will be passed to the customer, in an agreed format which should be documented in the contract. This will normally be by the provision of written reports within a number of days after the end of each time period, for review at progress meetings. For simple processes a form of exception reporting may be acceptable. It will form part of the review process at the management meetings, discussed further in Chapter 10. Both the customer and the supplier will be responsible for ensuring that the standards are maintained, with the supplier's obligation to observe them and the customer's right to check them.

Other statistics must be kept and reviewed from time to time in order to note whether the service levels in general are working successfully, whether an improved service would be feasible, and how future requirements will impact the existing services.

Incentives for performance

Once the service levels have been ascertained, the impact of failure to meet them must be assessed and the consequences defined in the contract. This can entail considerable negotiation. They must be acceptable to both parties.

It is important that any failures are resolved quickly before becoming accepted as being normal. There are many stages of remedying defective performance before resorting to the worst sanction of termination of the contract, which is a remedy to be invoked only when all else has failed. At that point the customer will be in an unenviable position.

If service levels are not being attained, it follows that there is a failure by the supplier in complying with the terms of the contract. As a result, the customer is getting less than has been agreed to be provided for the charges payable and should consequently not have to pay the full amount. The supplier may therefore be required to make payments or accept a remission in the charges if performance for critical services is below what has been agreed and yet the situation is redeemable so that termination of the contract would not be a necessary or desirable option.

Service credits, sometimes known as performance index rebates, and liquidated damages are the two approaches to this. Service credits, linked to critical service failures singly or in combination, represent a simple form of price adjustment for not achieving the contracted-for service. Liquidated damages are a form of compensation estimated in advance, denoting the foreseeable financial loss to the customer of breach of contract – in this case of more serious failure to provide specific services to particular levels. The principles of liquidated damages are discussed further in Chapter 14.

However, in outsourcing, financial recompense to the customer for the supplier's failure to meet the service levels while the contract continues in force is intended primarily to be a financial incentive for the supplier to maintain or improve the service levels by a threat of reduction in profits, rather than to be comprehensive compensation for the customer.

Service credits may be payable as fixed sums or treated as rebates to the charges. Liquidated damages will normally be expressed in terms of a sum or as a percentage or fraction related, for example, to a daily rate or other rate on which the charges are based, by adjustment to the charges payable or by cash payment by the supplier to the customer. If actual money is being paid out by the supplier, then terms of payment should be set out in the contract.

For example, liquidated damages may be payable for un-availability, over a period of time, of a particular critical service or constantly degraded response times. Service credits may be payable in respect of failure of individual measured services.

In practice, the distinction between service credits and liquidated damages can become blurred.

An overall performance index may be constructed as a technique for prioritizing the critical services and calculating the amounts due. First, an analysis of the services to identify the key activities crucial to the customer's business success will be necessary. The approach should be to focus on those measures which really matter and that are quantifiable and objectively measurable over defined time periods, such as accounting periods or month-by-month. Some services may be accrued over different business units or by site. A sample number of critical processes may be taken as being representative.

One method of proceeding is to draw up a worksheet for each vital service – or system or business function or product – according to how the service levels are categorized and defined. The worksheet will set out the function of that service and its impact on the overall business operation. The consequences of its failure to reach the agreed service levels need to be specified, and if possible quantified, taking into account any measures that would be pragmatically taken by the customer to minimize the extent of the lack of performance. For example, if the help line telephone line were out of action for a number of hours through the supplier's failure, an alternative telephone number could be established. All the users would have to be notified of the new telephone number and renotified when the original line is restored. Could the resource time of doing this be quantified and evaluated?

The worksheet should contain the calculations for the costs involved for internal purposes, as a reminder for the customer of the justification behind the figures.

An aggregate figure will be agreed to be available overall within any one year, rolling 12 months or other timeframe, to be applied for rebates, remission of charges or actual payment. This total figure will depend on the perceived level of risk, the basis of the charges and the profitability of the contract to the supplier and should be sufficient to act as an inducement for the supplier to restore performance, without being so large that it would in itself destroy the supplier's profit margins and create the risk of insolvency. Taking an extreme hypothetical position, if all the critical services failed to their fullest extent, accumulated over the period concerned, the total remission obtainable would be limited to this maximum sum. Of course, what would actually happen before this catastrophe occurred is that the disaster recovery procedures would have been implemented and various other practical measures taken because otherwise in this doomsday scenario, the customer would no longer be operating a viable business, and such a major failure would justifiably threaten the supplier's solvency. However, for incentive purposes, this is how the payments are worked out.

This amount should then be broken down by allocation among the critical performance standards, according to their relative value. This allocation is an artificial mechanism which may be based on formulae of greater or lesser complexity. For example, a weighting may be applied in calculating rebates payable in respect of any individual critical service in terms of its relative value to the others, or to some benchmark. Response times for a particularly important online process might be given a weighting of 20 per cent compared with a weighting of 1 per cent for speed of responses to a database enquiry system. It follows in this example that the organization regards the first process as 20 times more important than the second, which is far less critical, and that this would be reflected in the respective rebates proposed for failure of these particular services. The accumulated values of the rebates together form a weighted performance index.

It would not be relevant to create a coherent set of related performance indicators where the services and types of performances differ significantly.

Some allowance will normally be made for breaches of service levels before payments or rebates are triggered. This may take the form of:

- the achieved service level being less than the agreed service level by a set percentage before the service credit falls due
- the rolling period over which the performance is measured being greater than a single time period
- the unavailability of a service over a limited period of time
- an accumulated number of service level failures within a number of hours or within a single time period
- a distinction being drawn between minor and major variances to performance level. For minor variances, the parties will agree corrective action within a given timescale. If this does not lead to restoration of the agreed performance level, it automatically becomes a significant variance. A number of minor variances, or a single or small number of major variances, may therefore trigger a service credit in the accounting period concerned.

The supplier may argue that following payment or remission or rebate, the failure record should be cleared and the accumulation will restart. This may mean that, over time, unsatisfactory service levels are being maintained without being so bad as to trigger incentive payments. Consequently there may need to be a single incentive to raise the general level of performance. This could be formally reviewed less frequently than the normal measurement period – perhaps at the end of each year – and a sum set aside as remission to cover accumulated poor performance of this nature.

A failure or loss of service which occurs because of events outside the supplier's control and therefore not reasonably attributable to the supplier should be specifically excluded from the calculations for performance incentives in the contract. This is discussed at greater length in Chapter 14.

For loss of some services, it will not be possible to set a calculated, objective figure and yet, for the purposes of motivation, a small sum might be allowed as recognition of recompense. Thus, if a proportion of the charges are made for PC maintenance, in a particular installation lack of maintenance might have to extend to a large number of machines to have any critical operational impact. A service credit might then be agreed if the failure to maintain were to exceed a certain time period or number of machines despite the lack of quantifiable estimated loss.

Either service credits or liquidated damages may be selected for any particular failure, or they can operate together. If they are both to be included there should be a contractual provision to prevent them accumulating at the same time to create a double recompense in respect of a single ground of fault.

In addition to accepting the invocation of these payment criteria, the supplier should contractually commit to taking corrective action. Measures to address the source of the inadequate performance will be the primary action. Both parties may need to consider changing the service levels and/or the prices if in fact the service levels have been found to be unrealistic in practice.

There may also be a definition of 'material breach' if sufficient failures occur or if a single failure lasts for longer than a specified time; this entitles the customer to terminate the contract if the service level failures are so serious that this becomes necessary.

While service credits and liquidated damages are being negotiated, a supplier may seek positive motivation for exceeding service levels. But the customer is paying for those service levels it requires for its business. There will normally be no commercial benefit to the customer in enhanced service levels or, if there is, it will be an unlooked-for, even unnecessary, benefit for which the customer will not expect to have to pay.

Contractual documentation

If there is a large number or variety of services, they may be catalogued in a separate schedule in a document which is referenced from the services clause in the main body of the agreement. This will also be the most efficient way of allowing for an expansion of service provision during the life of the contract, as the schedule can be amended without affecting the agreement itself.

The service levels themselves, and the formulae used in establishing them, will also normally be in a separate document, or in several such documents, being the service level agreements which will be formally incorporated into the contract to be integral to it and legally enforceable.

The definitions of the services and service levels should be reviewed from a legal point of view. The wording should be unambiguous and readily understandable, and the requirements should be set out clearly. Tables and matrices may be appropriate.

The financial principles according to which the service credits or liquidated damages become payable are also normally articulated separately, as another schedule. This document must be related to the services and the service level agreements.

The format of the documents should facilitate amendments, enhancements, additions and deletions. There should be a front page for document change control, noting the dates and issue numbers of amendments and circulation. It may be helpful for each page to be dated and given an issue number.

The documents must be made available to those people who

are responsible for meeting the service levels, so that they know what is required.

Note

1   Supply of Goods and Services Act (1982).

6 Premises, equipment and human resources

Special considerations arise in those outsourcing arrangements where the customer's premises, equipment and staff are to become the responsibility of the supplier. In these situations legal advice from property and employment specialists will be called for. In this chapter some of the factors which will require consideration are indicated.

All outsourcing contracts concern the services which are to be carried out for the customer by the supplier to agreed standards. Some outsourcing transactions extend further than this. In those cases where the customer is handing over a large part, or the whole, of its IT capability for the supplier to run, the hardware, other equipment and assets used will be transferred to the supplier to use in the provision of the services. The supplier may acquire the customer's premises in order to continue to carry out the services. The customer's staff will become employees of the supplier. In such circumstances, the contract must therefore cover the legal issues involved in transferring the assets associated with the services from the customer's to the supplier's control.

Specialized financial advice will undoubtedly be beneficial in relation to the price being paid in connection with the business transfer. The allocation and apportionment of sums among the different categories of what is being transferred – including goodwill, if this is being regarded as a transferable asset – and the extent of any prepayments will be significant for taxation purposes, such as corporation tax and value added tax.

Not all outsourcing contracts will involve any business transfer features. The services can be carried out at the customer's premises on the customer's equipment, or located at the supplier's site with the supplier's existing hardware and communication systems. In other contracts, arrangements in relation to premises, computer equipment and human resources will be an integral part of the transaction.

Business transfer

If there is only a simple and limited transfer of assets of the business involved, the legal statement of the requirements may form sections within one single outsourcing contract document. It will be more manageable to create two separate, but related, contractual documents if the transfer of business assets is a significant part of the transaction. The services agreement will focus on the continuing outsourcing services. The business transfer agreement will cover the one-off transfer of the assets.

The business transfer agreement will state the price to be paid in respect of the assets: those which can be sold by the customer to the supplier; the leased interests; the third-party contracts; the intellectual property licences; the consumable stocks, such as paper and forms; and the records relating to the outsourced business activities. Certain assets will be specifically excluded: some records and third-party contracts; any book debts; sums to be recovered; and some retained assets.

On the agreed date, formal delivery will take place of the assets themselves and the executed agreements. Costs will be allocated to the customer before the cutover date and to the supplier afterwards, and apportioned as necessary for any period extending before and after that date.

The associated contracts falling under the overall aegis of the business transfer agreement are concerned with the transfer of various kinds of asset from the customer to the supplier: the property leases, hire contracts, assignments, novations, licences and insurances. The business assets which are owned by third parties, other than the accommodation, may be transferred to the customer by assignment or novation of existing agreements. The differences between assignment and novation are discussed in Chapter 2.

Third parties will not have the same commercial incentives or involvement as the customer and supplier in progressing the transfer of the agreements with any urgency. There is no reason to assume that all existing third-party contracts with the customer are satisfactory, and the supplier will have to examine the contents of these agreements systematically before taking them over. As to which of the parties should take prime responsibility for getting the consents and licences concerned in the transfers from landlords, equipment lessors and others, this will depend on the supplier's experience in negotiating with third parties on outsourcing-related transfers. It may be that the customer will be in possession of all the relevant information and in a better position to take control. Indeed, there may be confidentiality obligations requiring the customer to do so initially. In any event, the customer should be prepared to give an undertaking to act reasonably with regard to the existing contracts and to assist the supplier as necessary in the transfers, perhaps with reimbursement of expenses incurred by the supplier. Agreement must be reached as to who will pay any costs of obtaining consent from third parties and what is to be done if the consent is legitimately refused. It may take considerable time and much persuasion to sort matters out acceptably.

The customer will be expected to inform and consult with the supplier before the cutover point, mainly concerning any proposed action over employees being transferred, such as dismissal or variation of terms of employment, and to give assurances about the condition and ownership of those assets which it is treating as its own. At the same time it will limit its liability.

Other contracts which the business transfer agreement may encompass will be those between the customer and third-party end users of the services to be outsourced. The end users may be other legal entities within the customer's group of companies or independent companies, who still wish, or need, to take those services.

It may sometimes be practicable for the contract to be activated in stages. There may have been pressures to sign the contract by a particular date, whether for reasons of timing in order to meet an imposed deadline, or for financial or political imperatives, with cutover being deferred for a period. If so, these somewhat imperfect circumstances may allow a time-frame for those who are in charge of coordinating the negotiations to confirm all the linked contracts and sort out the service levels prior to cutover. Alternatively, a transitional period of weeks or months may follow the formal takeover before the date from which the contract becomes fully effective. It is often during this transitional phase that a number of outstanding issues are finalized.

If the contract is brought into effect in stages, it must be made conditional on success in reaching agreement on all the outstanding matters and subject to getting all the third-party contracts, licences and consents agreed. If any significant element fails to fall into place, it would be normal for the customer to expect to be able to terminate the contract without being obliged to compensate the supplier. However, failure in concluding the collateral agreements may be primarily attributable to the customer. In this case, negotiations may focus on the amount of compensation which would reasonably be payable to the supplier, and the contract should set out what is expressly agreed.

Premises

The outsourced services may be carried out at the supplier's premises or at the customer's premises, or at both in combination. If the services are to be performed at the customer's existing premises, the site may remain under the customer's control or, as part of the transaction, the supplier may take over the tenancy or ownership of the location. If the site is to be sold to the supplier, the right of the supplier to occupy the premises will continue independently of the outsourcing contract. On termination of the contract for any reason, the supplier will remain in ownership or possession.

A separate property contract will be negotiated if the supplier will be exclusively using, renting or buying the premises, giving the supplier a legal interest, whether by sale or formal lease or sublease or licence, for the purposes of providing the services. The terms must be negotiated, together with the sale price or rental or other charges. There will be a number of technical matters to work through, with the assistance of property lawyers.

In the case of assignment of the lease or a sublease, or where a licence is being granted and the customer is not the freeholder, consent from the original or current lessor to the lease or licence must be obtained. Any existing disputes between the customer and the landlord will give the landlord the opportunity of imposing conditions before granting its consent, and further assessing the desirability of having the supplier as a tenant, according to its financial stability and other relevant characteristics.

If the services are to be provided at the customer's location and the site will remain under the customer's control, the customer will remain responsible for the outgoings in respect of upkeep, insurance and maintenance. Heating, air-conditioning, electricity, physical security and cleaning are ongoing costs. Office furniture and equipment, faxes and telephone lines must be provided. The supplier should ascertain whether its staff will be able to use the general facilities available to the customer's employees. At the same time, the customer is entitled to insist that the supplier's staff will comply with security, health and safety regulations. There may be special rules about access and identity cards, or limits on the times during which access is permitted. The regulations may extend to standards of dress and of conduct, such as express anti-discrimination policies. These matters should be articulated in the contract.

Business assets

All the assets forming part of the transaction, including computer hardware and communications equipment, third-party contracts and software licences and possibly miscellaneous items such as furniture and consumables, must be identified by listing or describing them or otherwise, as part of the business transfer agreement. Those assets which might have been part of the transfer, but which are not included, should also be catalogued if there is going to be any doubt about them, to clarify the boundaries of what has been agreed.

A range of options in respect of asset transfer will be open to the customer in the outsourcing transaction. Different arrangements for transfer will follow according to whether the hardware items and other equipment – mainframes, PCs, workstations, communications hardware, servers, and so on – are owned or leased by the customer.

For those assets which are leased, the terms of the lease must be reviewed. It is likely that formal consents or licences will be needed from the lessors for transfer or assignment, or for the agreements to be novated by replacing the customer as party to the original agreement by the supplier. In these circumstances, although the lessors must be approached, they will have no incentive to be positively helpful or make swift progress, and may therefore need to be encouraged or pressured.

Before assets are transferred, the supplier should undertake a process of 'due diligence', closely examining those contracts entered into by the customer in respect of the assets, together with any connected procedures, in order to identify risks and potential future costs. Charges which may arise might be indirect or otherwise not obvious. For example, in relation to insurance costs which will become the responsibility of the supplier, the customer may have previously been able to obtain discount rates as a subsidiary of a larger group through bulk buying, or it may have previously self-insured.

Other ongoing contracts may be transferred with the necessary consents, such as those for support and maintenance and the software licences, the latter being discussed in Chapter 8.

The ownership of the equipment may remain with the customer which must then decide who is to manage it. The supplier may take over the management; this may include responsibility for making periodic payments to third parties for maintenance and insurance, taking over the existing maintenance agreements from the customer either at the date the outsourcing contract takes effect or at the point at which the agreements come up for renewal. Which of the parties has the better negotiating power to deal with the maintenance-providers? It may be a customer which is a large organization with a number of associated companies or an outsourcing supplier with many customers using the same equipment or software. The costs will be charged back to the customer, whichever of the parties is the negotiator.

Where equipment is replaced by the supplier, it may be doing so as agent for the customer in which case the equipment belongs to the customer, or in its own name but for exclusive use by the customer in the services. It may be a replacement by the supplier of any item of hardware, such as a computer, which will be used for a number of the supplier's other customers too.

The extent of the customer's involvement in the purchasing decisions in respect of equipment exclusively for its use should be clarified. The customer may expect to be consulted on the specification and financing and to know about what is being proposed in advance, or it may be content to leave the buying decisions entirely to the supplier.

When the outsourcing contract comes to an end, there may need to be an agreed procedure for selling to the customer any equipment purchased in the supplier's name for the customer's sole use, ideally at a previously agreed price formula. The transfer of these assets at the expiry or termination of the contract may be a material factor in assessing whether the legislation on staff transfer, as discussed in Chapter 7, will apply in respect of the staff concerned.

Human resources

The quality and continuity of the supplier's staff who are to deliver the services will be of immense interest to the customer which will have been assessing those of the supplier's personnel who have been put forward to respond to the invitation to tender, who have been making the presentations and giving assurances about what can be provided, and who are negotiating the contract.

Each party may wish to have some say in the appointment, or any replacement, of the other party's senior representatives, as the people in these roles will work closely together and will be crucial to the success of the outsourcing relationship. This is dealt with in Chapter 10. Tension may arise in the negotiations if the customer expects to be able to participate in the choice of successors to any staff of the supplier who leave, other than the personnel agreed as key to the outsourcing functions.

In general, the customer may need contractual assurances about the availability of sufficient suitably qualified and skilled staff, at the appropriate level for what is required, particularly if the charges for staff are directly levied on the customer so that payment will be for a number of staff at each of a number of levels of experience. The customer may reserve the right to veto the appointment of any staff on reasonable grounds, such as security if this is salient, and to exclude those who do not conform to agreed principles such as non-discrimination or compliance with staff regulations. In such cases, the customer may require the immediate replacement of any employee of the supplier who individually is found to be in persistent or material breach of the service obligations under the agreement, or in the case of reasonable suspicion of fraud, dishonesty or serious misconduct. This will be difficult for the supplier to resist.

Some continuity in the supplier's staff will reasonably be anticipated by the customer, so that payment is genuinely for the provision of services and not for duplication of effort or training occasioned by new personnel who have to learn the customer's ways of working. Quite reasonably, the customer does not want the supplier's staff to become experienced and knowledgeable in its applications and then to be moved elsewhere. Conversely, the supplier's staff will have a career structure and will move from post to post for promotion or to gain different experience. For key personnel only, it may be feasible to negotiate a minimum period for which they should be carrying out the work for the customer, a sufficient period of notice if it is intended to move them to different work, and the power to agree substitutes if changes are made. Nevertheless, there can be no absolute certainty about any particular individuals, who have their own careers to consider and may choose to resign and go elsewhere.

Staff working closely with staff of another employer may find that employer more attractive than their own. In a long-term outsourcing contract, or in selective outsourcing with no features of business transfer, either the customer or the supplier or both may be apprehensive about this. An employer may want to restrict recruitment of its employees by the company either for which or by which services are being provided respectively.

If this is an issue, a provision in the contract will give some limited protection. Employers are not entitled to impose restraints on ex-employees merely to protect their own competitive position. Employees are free to choose for whom they would like to work and cannot be prevented from responding to an open advertisement for employment as an independently considered career move. However, a carefully worded constraint clause will prevent active enticement by one party of the other's key personnel directly involved in the services being carried out for the duration of the contract. The safeguards in drafting an appropriate clause should include reasonable time limits (weeks or months, rather than years) and geographical restrictions. The individual circumstances of the employment situation will always affect what will be regarded as acceptable. The courts carefully scrutinize the extent of such restrictions in reviewing whether the actual wording used constituted what was necessary for an employer to protect its investment or whether it has gone beyond what was reasonable.

The responsibility for such employment matters as work permits, legal and other costs and taxation for the staff carrying out the outsourcing services must unequivocally be the supplier's as the employer of the staff.

Other concerns for the customer may arise over confidentiality, which should be covered by an express commitment by the supplier as discussed in Chapter 12. Chapter 13 suggests points which should be covered in the contract in relation to human resources when the contract comes to an end. The area of greatest legal risk in relation to staff arising in outsourcing concerns transfer of staff from the customer to the supplier. This is discussed in the following chapter.

7 Transfer of staff

This chapter concerns transfer of staff as part of the outsourcing process. Employees of the customer have particular legal rights in many outsourcing situations, and this is a major area of risk for the outsourcing supplier. The customer also needs to be aware of the issues which will be covered in the contract.

Not all outsourcing arrangements necessarily involve full-scale staff takeover, acquisition of computer equipment and a licence or lease of premises. Yet there may be deemed to be an automatic transfer of the customer's employees to the supplier at law without deliberate intention by either party, because of the legislation applying to business transfers, which may include outsourced services, and its interpretation in the courts. Up-to-date specialized employment law advice should therefore always be taken, particularly as the rules and their application are constantly changing as a result of case law.

Both the customer and the supplier should treat employment issues sensitively. It is not unknown for a potential outsourcing to be sabotaged by current staff. The knowledge that outsourcing is going to take place creates great uncertainties for staff, who may be anxious about what is to happen to them and worried about losing their jobs. As soon as staff learn that outsourcing is an option being considered, some of them may find other employment and resign rather than wait and see what will happen, fearful of suffering unwanted upheavals in their working lives. If key staff leave, it can become difficult for the customer to keep the IT systems running satisfactorily, making them less attractive for a supplier to take on.

However, some staff may welcome the opportunity to move to a new employer with enhanced career prospects and increased variety of work. The outsourcing, giving access to a wider range of computer career opportunities and broader training possibilities, may act as a catalyst to motivate them. An outsourcing supplier may have more of a vested interest than a user in keeping up with the latest technology and method-ologies and in educating employees to be flexible in acquiring new skills and responsibilities. The supplier may have been selected partly on the basis of its knowledge of the customer's industry sector. The adaptable employee who transfers with know-how gained from working in a specific kind of business will have useful expertise for the new employer and for a future career.

There are different ways in which staff may be invited to participate in the outsourcing process. Counselling and appraisal sessions may be set up. Some customers involve their IT employees in the choice of supplier by allowing them to express a preference as to which shortlisted supplier they would choose to work for.

For those staff being transferred from the customer to the supplier's employment, the customer must take account of the intangible and not easily quantifiable business risks of the loss of corporate experience – such as a loss of understanding the company's political nuances. This can make it difficult to envisage bringing the contract back in-house. Initially the staff transferred will share some identity with the customer organ-ization to which they used to belong. They will not need any training to understand the services being delivered and the context of those services. But their new career path will lie within the structure of the supplier's company, and their loyalties will change over time.

The EC Directive and UK Regulations

The subject-matter of this chapter arises from an EC Directive brought into effect for the purpose of safeguarding employees' rights when a business is transferred, known in short as the 'Acquired Rights Directive',[1] and referred to in this chapter as 'the Directive'.

A Directive is a law made to apply in all EU member states by means of legislation passed individually by each member state. The legislation which was brought in by the UK to implement the Directive is the 'Transfer of Undertakings (Protection of Employment) Regulations'[2] or 'TUPE' from the initials of the principal words, familiarly pronounced 'Choopy', since amended in certain respects.[3] It will be referred to in this chapter as the 'Regulations'.

European legislation within the European Union is a compromise among the varying political cultures and legal systems of the member states. Different legal systems in the member states have different approaches to employees' rights and to the ways in which legal decisions are made. The final court of appeal for member states is the European Court of Justice which looks at cases individually according to their specific facts. It also considers cases broadly from the perspective of the purpose of the legislation as a matter of social policy, to protect the rights of employees. This is the approach taken by many of the Continental legal systems. The results of cases adjudicated in the European Court of Justice may not easily be applicable in subsequent cases with different circumstances. The outcomes of cases determined in that court will nevertheless, by analogy, bind decisions made in courts in member states. The English courts, such as the Industrial Tribunal and the Employment Appeals Tribunal, make decisions in the cases which come before them by investigating the objective facts and considering the actual words used in the legislation, but will also have regard to the interpretative criteria laid down in cases which were decided in the European Court of Justice.

The purpose of the legislation

The purpose of the Directive is to protect the rights of staff on a change of employer when a business operation is transferred, by enabling the employee to continue to work under the same conditions as before. The effect is that the contracts of employment of protected employees continue after the transfer, the new employer being substituted for the former employer.

The legislation was introduced as a matter of public policy. Before the legislation, if the employer's identity changed, the contract of employment was brought to an end. A new employer would then be in a strong position to set employment terms and conditions for exactly the same job which were inferior to those under which the employee had previously worked. The employee would also have lost the rights accrued as a result of length and continuity of employment in redundancy or dismissal situations.

The original intention of the legislation was to protect employees from redundancy when their company was restructured, merged with another company or was acquired by another business. However, because of the actual wording in both the Directive itself and the Regulations, and the ways in which this has been interpreted by the courts, the application of the law has been extended, beyond what was originally contemplated when the Directive was first drawn up, to other situations, including outsourcing.

The Regulations provided what was perceived as being the minimum necessary to implement the Directive into English law. The words used in the Regulations do not entirely reflect the contents of the Directive, and this has meant in practice that the law is not clear. This has led to a number of cases coming before the courts in the UK to interpret both the Regulations and the Directive, to synchronize the differences and to conform to the requirements of the original Directive. Cases from the

UK, as from other member states, have also ascended through the appeal court hierarchy and have finally been decided in the European Court of Justice.

The courts' interpretation of the legislation will be discussed in this chapter to illustrate how the outsourcing situation may be affected, although the decisions are not about outsourcing IT services. This means that the cases themselves are referred to and are therefore identified in the endnotes in case further reference is sought. The legal position is evolving, and any cases reported since this book went to print may well modify or change the situation.

In this chapter the customer company will be referred to as the 'transferor' of the staff and the outsourcing company will be the 'transferee'.

What the Regulations say

The Regulations provide that:

- On the 'transfer of an undertaking', the contracts of employment of employees engaged in the undertaking immediately prior to the transfer are not terminated; instead, they *automatically* transfer on the same terms and conditions to the transferee of the undertaking as if originally made between the employee and the transferee. This means that an employee has the right for his or her employment to continue on existing terms and conditions.
- Any dismissal connected with the transfer is *automatically* unfair, unless there is an 'economic, technical or organizational reason entailing changes in the work force'. This means that an employee has the right not to be dismissed in connection with the transfer.
- Collective rights are also *automatically* transferred, and there are obligations to consult with employees' representatives in connection with the transfer. This means that employees have the right to be informed and consulted as to the way in which the transfer will affect them.

The Regulations do not apply to share transfers. The identity of the employer itself does not change, even if the share ownership does. They generally do not apply to sales of assets in themselves – for example, sale of land or plant alone. They will not apply to work awarded in-house under market testing or within government to another department or agency because there is no change to the legal identity of the employer.

In circumstances in which the Regulations do apply, at the point of transfer, the transferor's employees previously engaged in the undertaking concerned will immediately become employees of the transferee of the undertaking with or without any associated formal documentation, on their then existing terms and conditions, together with all of their accrued rights of continuous service (for example, redundancy rights, leave rights and so on) whether the transferee positively wants all the staff or not. This means that the staff will retain continuity of employment from the transferor. Modification of their terms and conditions will constitute grounds for a claim for constructive unfair dismissal (and will also be void). The transferee will bear any liabilities under the employment contracts taken over, including, for example, any costs of unfair dismissal compensation – or sex discrimination compensation, where there is no set limit on the amount which can be awarded.

Under the legislation, any former employees of the transferor laid off prior to contracting out because of the outsourcing will have a claim against the transferee. If either the transferor or the transferee dismisses anyone who was engaged in the undertaking before the time of the transfer, or shortly afterwards, then the transferee can be brought before an industrial tribunal for the unfair dismissal of that employee. An award will be made against the transferee for payment to the ex-employee. Reinstatement or re-engagement are also remedies (and might then include a requirement for back-pay).

If the employee is dismissed by the transferor prior to the transfer of the undertaking for a genuine economic, technical or organizational reason irrespective of the transfer, the liability for any successful claim for unfair dismissal will rest with the transferor. The transferor is still entitled to dismiss an employee on the grounds of actual misconduct in breach of the employment contract. If the reason for dismissal is redundancy, proper redundancy procedures should be followed to avoid the dismissal being unfair for procedural reasons. However, it is normally difficult to argue that redundancies are being made for an economic, technical or organizational reason if services are being outsourced to a supplier, and the same work still continues, having become the supplier's responsibility.

Cases have often arisen because, although a single redundancy or one unfair dismissal can be compensated, the principle may apply to many employees in a similar situation, all of whom would be entitled to compensation on the same grounds. In practice therefore, the outsourcing company must carefully examine the potential implications if staff are to be transferred.

What is an 'undertaking' and what is a 'transfer'?

The Regulations apply when an 'undertaking' – the word used – is transferred as what has been termed as being a 'stable economic entity'. An undertaking can be regarded as a 'business', but this does not mean only a self-contained business entity formally defined as such. The 'business' does not need to have been carried out for profit nor does it need to be a key part or otherwise a core element of the transferor's business.

It is not necessary for the whole of an undertaking to be transferred. Where part of a business is being transferred, the Regulations will generally apply where the part of the business being transferred is separately identifiable. It is immaterial if the services are incidental to the main business of the customer. There does not have to be any transfer of goodwill, capital assets or specialist know-how. The business will retain its identity on transfer if the new employer will be carrying out the same services as the old employer. IT services forming only a part of a business can therefore be an undertaking for these purposes. What is critical is whether the business section or division transferred retains its identity as a stable entity.

The European Court of Justice set out certain principles on what constituted a 'transfer of an undertaking' in a German case involving school cleaners, one of whom was Mrs Süzen.[4] She and seven of her colleagues were dismissed by a contractor when the school terminated its contract for cleaning services with that contractor and moved to another. Mrs Süzen claimed that the dismissal was invalid.

However, there was held to be no transfer under the Directive in the circumstances of this case. The Court confirmed that there must be a stable economic entity for transfer and added that the activities of the undertaking should not be confined to one specific contract. An 'entity' was defined as an organized grouping of people and assets facilitating the carrying out of economic activities for a specific purpose. An 'entity' thus implied more than the activities themselves. There had to be a transfer of the entity with its identity retained from the transferor to the transferee.

A number of factors must be considered together in assessing whether there is an economic entity, including: the type of business; whether there is a transfer of tangible or intangible assets; whether the majority of specially assigned employees are taken over by the new employer; and the degree of similarity of activities before and after the transfer. It was held that the Directive will not apply to the transfer of a service contract unless there is a 'concomitant transfer from one undertaking to the other of a significant tangible or intangible asset or taking over by the new employer of a major part of the workforce in terms of their numbers and skills, assigned by its predecessors to the performance of the contract'.

The presence or absence of assets was not of itself conclusive, however. In Continental law style, the emphasis is on taking all the various factors into account, including, here, whether there was a direct contractual relationship between the first contractor and the transferee. In the transfer of services from the customer to the outsourcing supplier there will normally be held to be a transfer for the purposes of TUPE. In a case decided by the European Court of Justice before Mrs Süzen's, also involving a German cleaner, Mrs Schmidt,[5] there was held to be a transfer in circumstances in which it might not have been thought that the principles would apply in practice.

Mrs Schmidt worked as a cleaner in a small savings bank in Germany. The bank was taken over. When the premises were renovated and cleaning services were contracted out to a firm responsible for cleaning the bank's other premises, Mrs Schmidt objected to a job at a higher rate of pay but with more work because the refurbished offices were larger. She said that her pay had effectively been reduced because she had more surface area to clean. Mrs Schmidt was the only employee involved. The same cleaning work continued to be required by the new employer. Yet, in this case, the European Court of Justice decided that the business had retained its identity. There had been a transfer of Mrs Schmidt's contract from the local bank to the larger group.

The English courts have to follow the principles established in these cases. The continuity of the working environment is a prime criterion – an 'operation actually continued or resumed by the new employer, with the same or similar activities'.

All those employees who were employed in the business immediately before the transfer of the undertaking to the transferee, (or those who would have been transferred had they not been unfairly dismissed) will transfer.

A 'transfer' of an undertaking will apply to management buy-outs, as it will apply to the transfer of a single contract and to a contract of services. There does not have to be a formal agreement or any document between the transferor and the transferee recording the transfer details.

The courts will investigate the objective circumstances surrounding the dismissal of an employee, to ascertain whether the transfer of the undertaking was the principal reason for the dismissal. The dismissal itself may be by the transferor or by the transferee, according to whether it has taken place before or after the transfer of the business.

Thus, for the Directive and the Regulations to apply, a transfer of a severable and identifiable economic entity, capable of being run as a business after the transfer, will constitute a transfer of an undertaking – which in many circumstances will certainly apply to first-generation outsourcing.

Further transfers

On the termination of the outsourcing contract, if the contractor loses the contract to a competitor, there will normally be no direct contractual relationship between the original outsourcing provider and the new supplier. If the services revert in-house, the outsourcing ceases. Thus in subsequent transfers, in either scenario, on the basis of Mrs Süzen's case the Regulations will not necessarily apply. The previous contractor does not cease to exist solely because it loses a customer and therefore there has been no transfer of an undertaking.

For TUPE to apply there would also have to be a direct transfer of significant assets at the same time, or the new contractor must take over a major part of the previous contractor's workforce. It is unlikely that anyone can know in advance if these conditions will exist on termination of the contract, in order for the situation to be addressed as part of the exit management arrangements which are discussed in Chapter 13. However, the supplier may require the customer to concur that assets no longer needed because of the termination should be transferred to the new supplier. It will then be up to the customer to agree with the new supplier that it will take on the assets.

An English case decided in the Court of Appeal involved a contract let by a health authority for the cleaning of hospitals and other buildings which came to the end of its fixed term[6] – a second-generation contracting-out.

After a competitive tendering exercise, the existing contractor, Initial Healthcare Services, lost the tender, and the contract was awarded to a new contractor, Pall Mall Services Group. Mrs Dines and other employees were made redundant when the services were handed back to the health authority at the end of the fixed term. Almost all the employees were taken on by Pall Mall, but on less favourable conditions. In the resulting case, the Court of Appeal held that the transfer of the cleaning contract to the new contractor constituted the transfer of an undertaking in two phases:

1 the handing back by Initial Healthcare to the authority of the hospital cleaning services, and
2 the award of the contract by the authority to Pall Mall of those services operated by 'essentially the same labour force'.

The staff, the services, the premises and the authority were all the same. The identifiable labour-intensive undertaking was the cleaning of the hospital. There were no differences in the technique or approach of the services being carried out. The transfer was effected by a series of transactions. It was decided that the Regulations applied to Mrs Dines, and she and her colleagues won compensation. The Court applied the principle that the employees' viewpoint had to be considered to give effect to the objective of the legislation – to protect the rights of employees.

Following Mrs Süzen's case, another UK case[7] involving second-generation contracting-out was decided in the Court of Appeal, taking into account the European Court of Justice decision. Helicopter services for oil rigs in the North Sea were transferred by Shell from one contractor, Brintel, to another, KLM. The transfer at issue was for one sector of the North Sea. KLM moved the Norfolk base from Beccles to Norwich. Some of the Brintel employees who lost their jobs contended that they should have been transferred.

The operation was not labour-intensive and did not involve the same staff before as after the transfer, as in the hospital cleaning case. As well as staff, there were significant assets of buildings, infrastructure and contracts which remained with Brintel. The Court of Appeal therefore held that there was an 'undertaking' but there was not a 'transfer' under the Regulations.

What these cases demonstrate is that the law is not yet fixed and remains uncertain in this area. Employees may face lack of job security. First-generation suppliers may acquire employees for whom they will have no work if the contract comes to an end and the employees do not move to the next contractor.

Transfer-connected dismissals

Dismissals related to the transfer of the undertaking will be unfair unless they can be shown to be for economic, technical or organizational reasons entailing changes in the workforce. An economic reason must relate to the way the business is conducted. Reducing long-term staff costs through making redundancies as a result of the transfer would not be an acceptable economic reason.

Vendors (especially receivers and other vendors of insolvent businesses) used to be able to sell a business without its workforce as a more attractive prospect for a purchaser. However, under this legislation it is not possible to avoid liability by dismissing employees before the transfer takes place: the dismissals will be regarded as unfair, as they will be connected with the transfer. The interpretation is that the employees would have been engaged in the undertaking if they had not been unfairly dismissed, and therefore their contracts of employment are deemed to have been transferred.

Any dismissals which result from collusion between the supplier and the customer will be considered to be transfer-connected dismissals and will thus come under the legislation.

Nevertheless, it has been held that *genuine* redundancies effected in a workforce after transfer may be justifiable. In these circumstances, ordinary unfair dismissal law applies, and people must be selected fairly for redundancy. Changes in the workforce may be required for economic reasons, and it is not always possible to safeguard the rights of workers. One case concerned the transfer of contracts to supply paediatric and neonatal services from two district health authorities to an NHS Trust. This was agreed to be a transfer as defined in the legislation. Two hospital consultant paediatricians received redundancy notices. They then applied for posts under the NHS

Trust and, on failing to get them, went to court.[8] The transferees had decided that it was necessary to create four new consultant paediatrician posts with different job descriptions. This was held to be a valid reorganization of the services, and the consultants' applications failed.

Thus it would be possible for the supplier organization to take the workforce and implement a redundancy programme if there were no longer any need for the work concerned because of 'some other substantial reason' – not simply the transfer of the business – provided that the redundancies were genuine and fair in themselves and complied with procedural requirements for consultation and selection.

A new employer would be advised to delay making changes until well after the transfer period to avoid the risk of any dismissals or redundancies being considered as transfer-connected.

Part-time or full-time employees

An employee does not have to work full-time to be affected. Part-time workers can be protected in the same way as full-time workers, and so too can those who spend only part of their working time in the undertaking concerned and the balance working elsewhere in the same employer's organization. This is demonstrated by a case in which a construction company, Amey Construction Limited, took over from a company in receivership, Farr plc, a number of employees who had been working on the majority of its contracts. Amey was found by an Industrial Tribunal to be liable for redundancy payments due to the other Farr employees, including their head office staff.[9]

Varying the employment terms

Generally, at law, employment terms may be changed only by agreement. An employee may agree expressly, or by implication, by continuing to work under the changed conditions.

However, an employee may later be able to sue an employer who relies on apparent acquiescence.

Contracts of employment may be terminated on economic, technical or organizational grounds at the time of a transfer which entails changes in the workforce, but may not be validly terminated if the reason for doing so is the transfer alone. The reason for making changes to the employment contract is therefore what counts.

The Regulations cannot be disregarded, even by consent. The reasoning is that the employees' rights arising out of transferred contracts of employment must be safeguarded by redressing the inherent imbalance of power in the employment relationship. It is not therefore legally permissible for an employee and the new employer to reach agreement that variations to the contract of employment will be acceptable following the transfer of the undertaking, simply because of the transfer. This applies even if there is some compensation for the variation, or if the transferred employee positively gives consent. The employee will still retain a right to make a claim to an Industrial Tribunal.[10]

Although such rights may not be waived under the legislation, an employee does have a fundamental legal right not to be compelled to work for an employer not of his or her choice. The employee may choose not to transfer to the new employer. But if the transferor is not willing to redeploy the employee, this constitutes resignation, not dismissal under UK legislation[11] which followed decisions taken in the European Court of Justice.[12] As a consequence, an employee who refuses to transfer will have the contract of employment with the transferor terminated but will then be left with no rights, losing any entitlement to redundancy or unfair dismissal.

Pensions

Occupational pension schemes are excluded from transfer.[13] At the point of transfer, accrued rights are frozen. The employee will have the option of taking a deferred pension, transferring funds into the transferee's scheme or into a personal pension fund.

With personal pension schemes, where the transferor is bound under the employment contract with the employee to make contributions into the employee's pension scheme, this obligation will also bind the transferee.

In practice many transferors ask the transferee to provide equivalent pension benefits. Any organization providing out-sourcing services to the government will be expected to provide pension rights or compensation 'broadly comparable' to civil service schemes.

Consultation

Where an employer is intending to transfer employees to another employer, meaningful consultations must take place, either with a recognized trade union or, alternatively, with employee representatives elected on an ad hoc basis or in advance.[14] The supplier must provide appropriate information in order to make the consultation practicable.

The consultation will be about the employees directly or indirectly affected, whether because they are going to transfer or because they will stay behind. It must include information on: the fact of the transfer; the reasons for it; when it is to happen; the legal, social and economic implications; and the measures planned in relation to the employees.

As recognition of trade unions is not a legal requirement in the UK, many customer organizations will have neither formal recognition agreements nor informal channels of consultation. In practice, non-unionized companies may arrange for a general standing body of employee representatives to be elected at the earliest opportunity, and certainly in advance of the formal outsourcing announcements. This will be a means of avoiding full publicity at any early stages of negotiations which may be regarded as sensitive and secret. It may be useful to explain the situation early on to the selected employee representatives in order to gauge likely reactions. The employers could agree with the representatives on the nature of the procedures for consultation and informing the staff.

Failure to hold consultations could lead to a complaint being presented to an Industrial Tribunal by the trade union concerned, employee representatives or affected employees. The deadline for bringing complaints is three months after the date on which the transfer was completed. Liability is up to four weeks' pay for each employee affected, which could include employees other than those directly concerned in the transfer.

What the Regulations mean in practice

If TUPE applies, the supplier will acquire all the customer's employees who provide the services being outsourced. A transferor undertaking which wishes to contract out part of its activities has the option of offering alternative employment to those of its employees who do not wish to be transferred. It may wish to retain in-house expertise. It may transfer to another part of its business any key staff it does wish to retain before the negotiations begin. Other staff may be moved into an area which is about to be contracted out. When investigating the services to be outsourced, suppliers should identify which employees will be transferred, how long they have been working in the business being transferred, and if there are any recent gaps in staff positions.

Any claim for unfair dismissal will be brought not against the transferor but against the transferee. The costs of unfair dismissal compensation will therefore fall on the supplier. This aspect of the contract is essentially a matter of risk evaluation and assessment for the supplier who, in determining the price, must build into the overall financial calculations an allowance for the potential financial liabilities, such as pre-existing employment liabilities.

The supplier is therefore justified in requiring access to staff files of those employees transferring and also in checking the standard of record-keeping in order to assess the risks of acquiring the customer's workforce for the outsourcing. It should also make enquiries about any changes in the workforce prior to the transfer, in case any employees who might otherwise have transferred have been dismissed and would be eligible to make a claim.

In any case in which the Regulations may apply, it is essential for the supplier to take specialist advice so that it may price the contract to cover for maximum legal risk, and to require warranties and/or indemnities against any possible historic pre-transfer liabilities. The risks are not simply those of non-compliance but the costs of subsequently deciding, perfectly legally, to change the structure of the workforce. As a matter of commercial negotiation, the risks may be split between trans-feror and transferee.

The supplier's pricing calculations will be based on the following maximum potential risks for each employee, encom-passing actual or anticipated losses:

- redundancy payment
- unfair dismissal compensation:
  - basic award, calculated in the same way as a statutory redundancy payment
  - compensatory award
- notice pay – generally up to a maximum of 12 weeks.

Future pensions liability may also be actuarially assessed and taken into account.

An employee, who currently must normally have two years' service before being entitled to make a claim for unfair dismissal, could take a case to the Industrial Tribunal in the first instance. There is generally a three-month time limit for making a claim, dating from the 'effective date of termination' of the employment. There are some exceptions at the discretion of the Industrial Tribunal, one of which is that it was 'not reasonably practicable' for the claim to be presented in time – perhaps due to ignorance of a matter which is essential to the claim. For example, it has been held that an employee who found out three months after her redundancy that someone had replaced her could not reasonably have brought her complaint earlier.[15]

In such circumstances, the time limit might then be related to the date on which an employee, apparently made redundant, actually became aware that a transfer was taking place or had taken place. This could be longer than three months from the date of termination of employment.

Where there has not been a dismissal, and the employee has apparently openly accepted employment with the new employer by transfer, but there are discrepancies in wages or salary, a claim may be brought several months after transfer to recover the difference in pay between the old and the new employment.

The contract

A list of employees to whom the Regulations may apply will be agreed between the transferor and transferee, for the outsourcing contract. The employee information in the Schedule will include:

- the number of staff who would be transferred if the Regulations applied
- the age and gender of staff, to calculate pension entitlements, details of salary and pay settlements
- information about existing terms and conditions, or references to where that information is to be found.

The supplier as transferee will need to ascertain the employment terms and conditions for all the affected staff. Terms and conditions may go back for many years and may themselves have been inherited from a previous employer, not necessarily through outsourcing but through acquisition or merger. Provision for acquiring the information must be made in negotiating the contract. The customer may give warranties and/or indemnities to the supplier in respect of the staff, for actions and omissions concerning employees prior to the transfer, in respect of claims for employment liabilities arising from the outsourcing, and about the accuracy of the information provided about the employees. The customer should confirm that proper consultation· with representatives took place. The supplier should indemnify the customer against claims by transferred employees arising after the transfer.

The contract should also entitle the customer to be given information about the supplier's staff at the termination or expiry of the contract. This information should be as much as is necessary for the invitation to tender for the next outsourcing contract, in case the Regulations apply to the transfer of staff from the old to a different contractor.

Future developments

There are some proposed amendments to the Directive.[16] More flexibility is sought, in order to ensure that the legal requirements do not threaten the survival of a business in terms of solvency, or make competition more difficult in the provision of services.

One proposal would make transferors and transferees jointly liable for breaches of obligations arising from the employment contract, or from other obligations in the employment relationship arising prior to the date of the transfer. An employee would therefore be able to bring an action against the former or the current employer in these circumstances.

Terms and conditions of employment will be able to be changed by agreement with employees' representatives in order to ensure the survival of the business transferred – this will be very relevant in the context of acquisitions of insolvent businesses, perhaps more so than for outsourcing.

It had been anticipated that the meaning of 'undertaking' would be made more specific, to clarify when the legislation applies, but the amendments which were proposed were not thought to be helpful. Thus, it will still be necessary to rely on case law to illuminate what 'undertaking' effectively means, and to clarify other controversial features of the Directive and Regulations.

Case law is still developing. Legal advice will be advisable, and indeed essential, in many cases. Ignoring the potential effect of the legislation on transfer of staff constitutes a risk for the supplier, and this risk should be allowed for in assessing the costs and pricing the outsourcing and by including the appropriate provisions, warranties and indemnities in the contract. The customer should limit its own risks by offering indemnities only to the extent that they are reasonable.

One reported anecdote shows the importance of analysing what the intended objectives of outsourcing are. One industrial equipment manufacturer outsourced because it was felt that the IT staff did not have the technical skills necessary to implement a new computer architecture. Yet in the outsourcing those same IT staff were transferred to become employees of the supplier. The manufacturer had not solved the underlying problem and the whole arrangement failed. The customer's unqualified staff became the supplier's unqualified staff.[17]

Notes

1   EC Acquired Rights Directive 1977 (77/187/EEC) ('on the approximation of the laws of Member States relating to the safeguarding of employees' rights in the event of transfers of undertakings, businesses or parts of businesses').

2   1981.

3   s33, Trade Union Reform and Employment Rights Act 1993, Collective Redundancies and Transfer of Undertakings (Protection of Employment) (Amendment) Regulations 1995 (SI 1995 No. 2587).

4   *Ayse Süzen* v. *Zehnacker Gebaudereinigung GmbH Krankenhausservice and Another*, ECJ Case C-13/95.

5   *Schmidt* v. *Spar und Leihkasse der Fruheren Amter Bordesholm Kiel und Cronshagen* [1994] IRLR 302.

6   *Dines and Others* v. *Initial Healthcare Services Ltd (1) Pall Mall Services Group Ltd (2)* [1994] IRLR 336.

7   *Betts and Others* v. *Brintel Helicopters Limited (trading as British International Helicopters) and Another*, Times, 1 April 1997.

8   *Porter & Nanayakkara* v. *Queens Medical Centre* [1993] IRLR 486.

9   *Rolfe* v. *Amey Construction Limited* COIT 5/124/148.

10   *Wilson* v. *St Helens Borough Council, Meade and Baxendale* v. *British Fuels Ltd*, Times, 18 July 1997.

11   Trade Union Reform and Employment Rights Act 1993.

12 *Katiskas* v. *Konstantinidis* (1), *Skreb* v. *PCO Stauereibetrieb Paetz & Co. Nachfolger GmbH* (2), and *Schroll* v. *PCO Stauereibetrieb Paetz & Co. Nachfolger GmbH* (3) [1992].

13 *Walden Engineering Co. Limited* v. *Warrener* [1993] IRLR 420; Regulation 7 of the Regulations, Article 3 of the Acquired Rights Directive.

14 Article 6, EC Acquired Rights Directive 1977, Collective Redundancies and Transfer of Undertakings (Protection of Employment) (Amendment) Regulations 1995 (especially Regulations 10 and 11) SI 1995 No. 2587.

15 *Machine Tool Research Association* v. *Simpson* [1988] IRLR 212.

16 On going to press, the latest information available is the Amended Proposal for a Council Directive Amending Directive 77/187/EEC on the Approximation of the Laws of the Member States Relating to the Safeguarding of Employees' Rights in the Event of Transfers of Undertakings, Businesses or Parts of Businesses.

17 Leslie P. Willcocks and Guy Fitzgerald (1994), *A Business Guide to Outsourcing IT*, Business Intelligence Limited.

8 Software

Rights of ownership and use of the software involved in the IT services are intangible, valuable and vulnerable to being overlooked in the outsourcing contract.

The origin of the various software used by the customer's IT department for the purpose of running its systems is likely to vary. It may have been designed and coded by the customer's staff. It may have been written partly by employees and partly by freelance contractors, or it may have been commissioned externally. It may have been acquired from, or licensed by, a third-party owner or distributor of the software. It may be a simple packaged product supplied in volume to numbers of users, or it may be highly customized or uniquely designed for the customer's business requirements. An important part of the process of negotiating the contract is to ensure that the software not owned by the supplier, or transferred to it, is correctly licensed for use by the outsourcing supplier and that the ownership is defined. The ways of dealing with software which will in future be used in the outsourcing must also be considered. Before an IT outsourcing contract is finalized, the licensing arrangements for all the different software need to be agreed.

Once the outsourcing is in operation, the supplier will be using the software in order to operate systems, process data and generate results. The supplier must have proper authorizations granted by the different owners of the software in order to have the rights to run the various software packages and systems legitimately. Authorization is normally demonstrated by means of licence documents which grant permission for use of the software under specified circumstances and impose stipulations to circumscribe that use.

It is possible, but relatively unusual, for existing licences to the customer from third-party software suppliers to be drafted widely enough to cover use for outsourcing. However, the situation must be investigated for all the software comprised in the systems. This review normally involves substantial effort.

The first part of this chapter outlines the reasoning behind the contractual provisions which should be made in respect of the software. An explanation is given of what is meant by owner-ship rights in software, so far as this is relevant for the purposes of the outsourcing contract. It describes what entitlements are conferred on the owners of the rights, and how they come into effect; how use of software is validly permitted; and the assurances which will normally be given by the software owner to the user.

Next are considered the different arrangements which should be made for: software belonging to the customer itself; software owned by third parties; any software owned by the supplier which the supplier will be using for the benefit of the customer; and, finally, any software developed in the course of out-sourcing.

The ownership of the software carries implications for the ways the rights to use the software are obtained. Software used in the customer's organization may belong to the customer itself, having been developed in-house, or because the customer has acquired the rights of ownership by assignment, perhaps having specially negotiated the rights for software which was specially commissioned. However, there will typically be many different kinds of software, not owned by the customer, which are needed for running the customer's IT operation. This software will be in use under licences granted to the customer by third parties who either own the software themselves or who have themselves been authorized by the software owner to grant licences.

In IT outsourcing, the supplier must have the right to run all the software, whether at the existing site or at a new site. It must also be clearly entitled to run software owned by the customer. For third-party software, the supplier as user must be licensed by the third-party software owner.

In general, the outsourcing supplier will be taking over responsibility for the software. It will be paying licence fees and maintenance and support charges to third-party owners or other licensors. It will be implementing the upgrades and new versions. The costs to the supplier of doing this, and the fees themselves, must be factored into the overall charges or identified as separate chargeable items. The customer should seek indemnities from the supplier against software misuse, whether by the supplier itself or by a third party, through the supplier's carelessness or lack of security.

What are 'rights' in software?

Those who own property of any kind have legal rights enabling them to protect their ownership. Software as property is of a kind specifically known as 'intellectual' property. This form of property which cannot be seen or touched, and which comes into existence through some kind of creative effort, also exists in graphics, music, plays and novels, amongst other works. The legal way in which this kind of property is protectable in the UK is by means of the intellectual property right of copyright. (Software which is business-specific or otherwise sensitive or belongs in a category of 'trade secrets' may also need to be legally protected through confidentiality agreements.)

Copyright is a right which is derived from legislation and which is applicable within a legal jurisdiction. Thus, in the UK, it is a right created by Acts of Parliament and statutory instruments.[1]

Other countries, in Europe, the USA or anywhere else, will have different ways of defining copyright under their laws and protecting software as property – if it is protectable at all under the legal system of the jurisdiction concerned. Copyright is the most usual way in which software is protected, but the features and applicability of copyright will differ from territory to territory. There are international treaties to facilitate trade, in which agreement has been reached over particular features which will be carried into the laws relating to copyright in force in the signatory countries. It is the features of copyright applicable to software within the UK which are described here.

Entitlement to copyright is limited in time, to 70 years following the death of the author, when the property will form part of the author's estate. Clearly, this is an unimportant limit at present as far as software is concerned.

Copyright protects 'original' work which has been recorded in some medium, whether visual, aural or electronic. For software, this does not mean that the coding needs to be especially innovative. It means that some individual contribution and effort has gone into producing it. Copyright is an economic right arising automatically without any formalities such as registration. It is the exclusive right of the copyright owner to copy, to issue copies or to adapt the copyright work, and consequently to prevent others from copying. 'Copying' means reproduction in any material form. Running off another copy of the software on disk or storing the software by electronic means constitutes copying just as much as photocopying or copying lines of code by hand. 'Adapting' includes modifying or translating the software, so that it may not be converted into another computer language or code without the software owner's permission.

It is not possible to use software without copying it, electronically or in hard copy. As an economic right, copyright is therefore a means for software publishers and value-added resellers to gain financially by making profits through licensing the software in order to recoup the investment which they have made in developing it.

There is a problem in practice in interpreting the level at which the law operates to protect intellectual property works. This causes uncertainties in the application of copyright to software. The copyright in a novel will prevent anyone from legitimately copying, translating or adapting the words of the novel without permission. It would also prevent the structure of the unfolding of the storyline being copied, even if the words used were entirely different. But the plot itself at its most basic level is not protectable. At the other extreme, if there is only one way in which an idea may be expressed, such as a mathematical formula, copyright may not be successfully claimed for it. For software, similar functions may be performed by quite separate programs, where the respective programmers have each used completely different coding. It may nevertheless be claimed that the program written later is an infringement of the first, and that the structure and functions have been copied. This is known as the 'idea/expression' dichotomy, or 'look and feel'. If an allegation of copyright infringement is made about a piece of software which is not a straight copy, expert evidence – necessary for all copyright infringement proceedings if copying is not admitted – will be required to determine whether, on the balance of probabilities, copying has in fact taken place.

The work preparatory to software publication, the flowcharts, user requirements, design specifications and program specifications will also be subject to copyright.

The value in intellectual property rights is difficult to assess, and the book value may be much less than the value representing the investment made in its development and its market value relating to its scarcity, originality and functionality.

Who owns rights in software?

The first owner of copyright in software is its author, unless the author is an employee and wrote the software in the course of his or her work, in which case the author's employer will be the first owner. Note that a self-employed contractor or a consultant from an external agency or a freelance programmer, in providing services to an organization, is not an employee of that organization. They will therefore retain copyright in the work they do if there is no agreement to the contrary. Although there will be an implied right for that organization to use the software for which it has paid, neither the commission itself nor payment for the work entitles that organization to ownership of the software. Where more than one programmer has contributed to the software development or where members of a team have collaborated in writing the programs, and the contributions are not distinct, there will be joint ownership. A system which consists of a collection or combination of individual programs and modules may belong to more than one copyright owner, and the combination or collection may itself be separately subject to copyright.

Where a number of freelance programmers are working on constituent parts of commissioned software, they may not individually be able to make any practical use of their own coding. However, their client who commissioned them may wish to enhance or update the software at a later date, or to market it commercially. Ownership of the resulting software will be much more useful to the client in these circumstances than to the contractors, if the design and coding is unique to the software concerned. Copyright can be transferred to another party by means of a formal agreement assigning the rights to the new owner. The contract for a contractor's services may therefore include assignment of the software which the contractor has been retained to write as part of the services being provided. Individual consultants or contractors will hold copyright in the work which they produce if this assignment provision is not part of their contractual terms. In any event, they should not automatically sign their rights away if they are not providing exclusive services or if the client is going to gain no practical advantage from them doing so. If the contractors have particular routines or modules which they use again and again, they should certainly hold on to copyright.

Permission to use the software

Commercial software developers, publishers and distributors will not rely on basic legal copyright alone in marketing and supplying software. They will expect their customers and end users to enter into contractual arrangements for use of the software by means of software licence agreements. A licence will give the owner the opportunity to impose conditions in an effort to control and restrict authorized use of its profit-making asset. For example, the software will be limited to use only on a designated computer at a particular location or a specified business environment and for a specific number of concurrent end users. It must not be copied except under the conditions permitted in the licence; it must be kept confidential; and it must not be accessed by anyone other than the licensee. To a large extent, the licence fee will be related to these restrictions, to enable the licensor to charge additionally for an increase in the number of concurrent users or an extension to further sites or as a result of a machine upgrade.

Since software cannot be used unless it is copied electronically, there is no accidental way of acquiring the right to use it. Software licences will normally not extend automatically to outsourcing arrangements.

Whatever the licence states, a licensee has the right to make a copy for back-up purposes, and, in certain limited circumstances, a licensee would have a right to decompile the software. This latter right is exercisable only as necessary in order to obtain information required to create another independent program which needs to operate in conjunction with the software from which the decompilation is being carried out. The intention of this right, which resulted from EU legislation with the purpose of enhancing free trade and competition, is to enable new interoperable (but not substitute) software to be created without permitting the misuse of third-party proprietary information in creating competing products.[2]

Using software without permission

To relate the general principles of copyright to outsourcing, the customer would be breaching the terms of its software licence agreement if the outsourcing supplier were allowed to access the software without proper authorization, and the outsourcing supplier would thereby be liable for unauthorized access to the software. This will be the case if the customer continues to take the licence in its own name and pay for it, but the software is being accessed and used by the supplier under an outsourcing arrangement, without the licensor's knowledge and consent.

A software licensor may legitimately object to the licence terms being varied for outsourcing purposes. Two principal reasons would lie behind such an objection. First, the outsourcing supplier may be a competitor of the licensor. Both of them may be in the same outsourcing market. In this situation the licensor would seek to create conditions to prevent the outsourcing supplier abusing its access to the software. Second, the licensor has to protect its investment in developing the software. The licensor will normally permit the outsourcing supplier to run the software provided that the licence fee is increased for this use.

Without the licensing permissions in place, a customer would risk the rightful owner taking legal action against it for damages for breach of its current licensing conditions. The outsourcing supplier would also risk criminal liability for using software without proper authorization.

Administrative exercise

The earlier in the contractual process that the software negotiations with licensors are initiated, the better. The review of licensing contracts, drafting assignments and agreements, and negotiating the transfers with third-party licensors, will probably involve far more time and effort than most customers would anticipate.

It is normally a major exercise to analyse the rights and restrictions in existing software licences. It is rare for all the customer's current software licences to be systematically gathered together in one place. It is relatively unusual to find a system of administrative review already established to ensure compliance with the requirements as set out in the licences – the number of copies allowed to be made, authorized access, confidentiality, and other conditions laid down by the licensor.

Employees may be unaware of the obligations set out in the software licences. They may not appreciate what the licence conditions state. The owner of the software may be unknown to them. This is the time to find out.

As part of this exercise, the support and maintenance contracts relating to the software should also be assembled and reviewed, ready to be discussed with the supplier.

The customer's software licences

For software owned by the customer, it will be a simple matter for the supplier to be given express permission to run the systems using that software by means of a licence within the outsourcing contract. If the customer has developed its own software using in-house staff, or if it has acquired rights of ownership to bought-in software by assignment, or if the software has been developed by external contractors for the customer under contracts for services which have assigned the contractors' rights in the software to the customer, there will be no problem for the supplier in using that software in the outsourcing, since no third party will be involved.

The customer must formally grant a licence to the supplier, as a provision in the agreement, stating that the supplier is licensed to use the customer's software for the purposes of providing the outsourcing services. The supplier should agree, by means of formal wording in this clause, not to use the software for any other purpose, not to disclose it other than for the performance of the services, and to acknowledge its

confidentiality. These would be the minimum requirements.
The customer may also require assignment to it of copyright of
any modifications and enhancements made to the software by
the supplier as part of the services. It would also be normal for
the customer to provide the supplier with an intellectual
property rights indemnity, as discussed below.

A licence is preferable to a once-and-for-all assignment of the
software by the customer to the supplier. Strategically, it is in
the customer's interests to retain ownership of its key systems
and applications. In principle they have an asset value to the
customer's company, and the supplier does not need absolute
ownership – it will not be intending to exploit the software
commercially. Principally, the software rights should be
retained because, when negotiating the outsourcing contract,
the customer should always bear in mind that there is the
possibility of the arrangement with the supplier coming to an
end in the future. In this event the customer will still need to
use its software. There is no need to hand over ownership of its
software assets to a supplier.

Intellectual property rights indemnity

A professionally drafted software licence will normally include
an indemnity from the owner of the software to cover the
possibility of any third-party claim of infringement being made
against the licensee legitimately using the software under the
terms of the licence. An example might be where software,
developed by the customer using its own staff and contractors,
is licensed by the customer to the supplier to run for outsourcing purposes. A third-party contractor who had worked
for the customer might have written the software without
assigning copyright to the customer at the time of carrying out
the programming services. The contractor subsequently dis-
covers that the software is valuable and being used successfully
and makes an allegation of infringement, asserting authorship.
Going back to the definition of copyright, the claim would not
be made out of possessiveness. It would be made because the

claimant believed that he or she had an entitlement to a share in the economic value being derived from the software.

If there were to be a valid claim, an injunction might theoretically be obtained to prevent future use of the software by the supplier, or the supplier might be liable in damages or for payment of royalties. It could be expensive for the supplier to counter the claim, in terms both of effort and of legal costs. After all, in this situation, the supplier would be an innocent party, using the software only to meet the customer's outsourcing requirements. The customer will therefore recognize its responsibilities by means of a limited indemnity in licensing the software.

An intellectual property rights indemnity in a software licence normally limits the licensor's liability to the licensee and is subject to some control by the licensor over the claim being made; it is in the licensor's interest to take over the defence to any legal action since the subject-matter of the claim is an asset belonging to the licensor. Similarly, the indemnity which the supplier should expect the customer to provide in respect of its own software will not necessarily be so extensive. It will indemnify the supplier against any expense, loss or damage as a result of any claim that the supplier's use of the customer's software under the outsourcing contract infringes the intellectual property rights of a third party.

Third-party software licences and support

A customer may use software continuously or regularly, but this does not mean that it will have the right to deal with this software as it chooses.

Licences to the customer for bought-in software or for software developed for it by a third party will contain a number of restrictions on use by the customer, as discussed earlier. Use will normally be confined to that customer – which would not necessarily extend to the customer's subsidiaries or associated companies – and the licence will normally prohibit any other party from using the software. This enables the licensor to retain control over the software comprising its intellectual property and prevent the risk of it passing to a competitor.

The choice for the licensor is to transfer, or extend the rights in, the original licence to the outsourcing supplier. Use of the software may be unchanged, or there may be a wider or different use of the software on account of the outsourcing.

Some licensors see outsourcing as an opportunity to increase their revenues, and will charge relatively high fees for the assignment or transfer of licences to the outsourcing supplier. They may do so even where the software will in fact be running on the same machine, in the same building, linked with the same systems as before, and operated by the same staff. The terms of their licences with the customer may well cover their rights to do so. Support costs for the software may also be affected.

Nevertheless, the licensors of this third-party software must be informed of the imminent outsourcing situation, so that the supplier may acquire the appropriate permissions to run the software legitimately.

If the charges being imposed appear to be excessive, the customer must consider its options. It is strongly advisable to sort matters out at this stage, although it can take much longer than envisaged to do so to everyone's satisfaction. The permissions should ideally all be in place when the outsourcing contract is signed or, at the latest, when the contract comes into effect, if these dates are different. If they are ignored, the risk is that the licensor will take legal action against the customer for the extra payment, or even in order to prevent the continued use of the software by the customer or the outsourcing supplier, or to bring court proceedings for infringement of copyright since the use would be beyond what was permitted in the original licence to the customer.

The customer must decide whether the software is really critical to its business. In the short term, it is almost inevitable that there will be no realistic alternative way of managing the business requirement.

From the customer's perspective, it may apparently be helpful if the outsourcing supplier can take on the responsibility for negotiating with third-party software owners. This is likely to be something which the supplier has experience in doing as a matter of course in setting up outsourcing arrangements, and which it will know how best to approach. However, the costs will be passed on to the customer and may be higher than the customer would have been able to negotiate.

Sometimes, if other customers are using the same software, the outsourcing supplier has its own licences for this purpose. In this situation, the supplier will already have negotiated with the licensor the opportunity to use the software for the systems of a number of its customers. The licensing fees can be spread over the customer base.

With important software and exorbitant demands there may be competition issues that could be raised if the software owner causes difficulties. Legal action can be considered by the customer and/or supplier against the software owner, on the grounds of unfair trading – to the Office of Fair Trading – or unfair competition – by complaint to the European Commission.

For example, under Article 86 of the Treaty of Rome – EC law directly applicable within the UK – a company with a dominant position in the marketplace is not permitted to abuse its position if trade between member states would be affected.

It is not simply that a company has a position of strength, but is a question of it taking unfair advantage of its position. A specialist software supplier which requires a high fee for a licence may therefore be setting its own agenda without having to take into consideration competitors, customers and ultimately consumers.

In establishing whether an undertaking is in a dominant position, the relevant market for the supply of particular goods or services must be defined. Are there other software packages available to the customer and supplier which could be regarded as reasonable substitutes for their similarity in function and price? A company would probably be regarded as having a dominant position if its share of its particular market was over about 70 per cent. There have been a number of instances where companies with much smaller market shares have been considered 'dominant'. Where the share is less than 50 per cent, the structure of the market will be important, particularly the market share held by the next largest competitor. A supplier of specialized software may thus be dominant in its market share.

Behaviour which would be considered abusive in this context when entered into by dominant firms might include: directly or indirectly imposing unfair purchase or selling prices or other unfair trading conditions; and making contracts subject to acceptance by the other party of supplementary obligations which have no connection with the subject of such contracts. An unfair price for the transfer of the software licence could therefore be questioned by the customer and/or supplier. Thus the Commission may be able to regulate an obvious case of an abuse of a monopoly position by an owner of intellectual property rights. Fines for non-compliance can be imposed, raised in aggravated circumstances or reduced to take account of attenuating circumstances, although the Commission will often try to reach consensus without resorting to the imposition of fines.

There have been a number of cases in which the software owner has taken legal proceedings against the supplier for copyright infringement in outsourcing situations, but in the UK they have been settled before actually reaching court.

From a practical point of view, valuable attention may be diverted from the time-consuming process of negotiating the outsourcing contract by having to take resources and effort to deal with the vendor of the software, with the concomitant risks of confrontation and costs. However, awareness of the European competition angle may be a useful point to discuss in any negotiations with large software vendors who appear to be recalcitrant, if there is no substitute for using their software.

For third-party software, the ideal time for the issues to be addressed is long before the outsourcing negotiations are in hand. If outsourcing is known to be a possible future option for the IT department, the matter should be raised when licence terms and conditions are negotiated for the procurement of new bought-in or specially commissioned software. This is the point when the customer's position will be at its strongest – when it has a choice of whether to take the software or to find an alternative.

As part of the original terms of supply of the software to the customer the licence may be expressly extended to allow for a future outsourcing situation; this prevents the need for any further negotiation between the licensor and the customer.

The supplier's own software

Third-party software may include the supplier's own proprietary software, which the supplier uses in providing or managing the outsourcing services. If the software becomes indispensable, there is a risk of reliance on it; this could rebound to the detriment of the customer at the expiry or termination of the contract. The software should be licensed to the customer, ideally in terms permitting its use beyond any possible termination of the supplier's services and for licensing of a future service provider. The customer should try to negotiate ongoing rights to use the source code of the software or for the source code to be held independently by an escrow agent, as discussed later. It would then be available to the customer in the event of failure of the supplier's business or if the supplier defaults in providing the services.

Software developed in the course of outsourcing

The contract should be clear about ownership of both new software and enhancements developed by the supplier during the outsourcing process. The customer would normally expect to acquire ownership of additions, enhancements and modifications to its own software, and to ensure that there is comprehensive documentation by the supplier as they are implemented. If the outsourcing contract should be terminated, the customer will still need the software.

Change of software during the contract term can be one of the most difficult areas in practice. For example, a supplier may choose to abandon the customer's proprietary software and substitute third-party software, justifying this on grounds of efficiency. Does the customer have any say in this decision? What rights in the new software to take effect at the end of the contract term can be negotiated on behalf of the customer?

Documentation

Systems and procedures manuals and other documentation should not be ignored in the consideration of copyright. The same principles will apply, although they will be simpler in practice and negotiation is likely to be less fraught. It may be necessary to make a number of user manuals available for the benefit of end users. Customers should be expressly entitled in the contract to use the supplier's documentation.

'Escrow' (source code deposit)

For some systems, neither the supplier nor the customer will have access to the source code.

Licences for third-party software in a typical installation will be for the software in object code or interpreted format, which will be satisfactory in the ordinary course of events for run-time operation. The source code is the human-readable format which theoretically enables an experienced programmer with expertise in the language in which the code is written to understand the structure of the program and the way in which it works after compilation or interpretation to achieve its application objective.

Thus, for software which needs modification and enhancements from time to time, or which interfaces with other software which may be upgraded, access to the source code is essential. However, this access would not inevitably be required by the customer. Provided that the licensor of the software or the third-party maintainer has that access, whether by ownership or by source licence, in normal circumstances it will be of no concern to the customer that it is itself prevented from holding a source licence. By discriminating in this way, the owner will be seeking to protect its assets and keep its rights to the source code to itself, providing support and upgrades as necessary from time to time.

Escrow agreements are a means of guarding against the consequences of the insolvency of the software owner, when support provision would cease. They may be negotiated with the software owner in circumstances where neither the supplier nor the customer has access to the source code. A copy of the source code will be deposited with a neutral third-party custodian for release only in certain situations prescribed in an escrow agreement between the software owner and the third-party custodian to which the customer or licensee would also be a party. The normal situation for release would be the insolvency of the third-party software supplier – not unusual in the volatile IT industry. If this happens, any commitment made in advance by the software supplier to its customer to make the source code available would not be guaranteed to be enforce-able against a liquidator. This is because the liquidator would have taken over the assets of the company, including the asset of the software source.

The insolvency will be therefore an event which triggers the release of a copy of the software source by the third-party custodian to the customer, to enable support and enhancements to continue to be provided until a purchaser is found for the software assets of the liquidated software company. Finding the appropriate programming knowledge and experience in under-standing the source (in the state in which it has been deposited) in order to amend it may be more of a wistful hope than achievable in practice. Nevertheless this is the way in which source code deposit or 'escrow' has developed in the software industry.

The wording of existing escrow agreements relating to the software should be reviewed, to ensure that the benefit would continue to be available for the outsourcing supplier. New software, licensed during the outsourcing, must be considered for escrow arrangements to permit access in the event of insolvency, and also possibly in the event of failure by the software owner to maintain it. Suitable provision should be set out in the contract for this.

The supplier should also agree to put the source code of its proprietary software used in the outsourcing into escrow, to guard against its own insolvency – when there would be other pressing concerns for the customer – or for passing the source code to the customer on expiry or termination of the contract.

Conclusion

Software licensing must be addressed early on in the out-sourcing contract. The customer needs to collate information about the current owners of its software and on the terms and conditions on which the software is licensed. This can be a lengthy procedure.

Software licences affect the outsourcing costs because software houses take the opportunity to charge for assigning their licences. Arrangements must be clarified for third-party software, the customer's software, the supplier's software and software developed, enhanced or modified during the term of the outsourcing.

Notes

1   Principally the Copyright Designs and Patents Act 1988.
2   Directive on the Legal Protection of Computer Programs ('Software Directive') 91/250 EEC OJ 1991, L122/42 implemented in the UK by the Copyright (Computer Programs) Regulations; SI 1992/3233.

9 Costs and charges

Costs will always be one of the drivers in the customer's move towards outsourcing, whether or not savings over present IT costs are the customer's prime objective. IT expenditure which is foreseeable and manageable may be an additional or alternative target. Whatever the reasoning, the customer will be intending to get value for money. In principle, with outsourcing, the costs should become more transparent and therefore more controllable. Cost reduction should never be the sole criterion for selection of an outsourcing supplier.

Outsourcing experience varies as to whether customers obtain the expected financial benefits or lose out. Whether the charges made over the life of the contract are as predicted and whether savings are achieved will be affected, first, by the way the contract is negotiated and finally worded, and, second, by the extent of changes to the services during the life of the contract.

Any invitation to tender or other opening request to an outsourcing supplier will always ask for proposals on charging. The different bids put forward will be considered and compared at an early stage in the selection process. Yet, because of the details involved and the links with other parts of the contract such as its duration and the service levels, the detailed charging arrangements may become one of the last matters on which agreement is reached.

According to the extent and nature of the services to be provided, the negotiation processes may be complex and precision of expression in the contract hard to attain. A combination of charging methods may be included in one contract, for different features of the services, drawn from a variety of pricing structures and costing mechanisms. In such cases, with numerous, complicated or lengthy formulae or calculations, it will be practical to set out the details of the charges independently of the body of the contract in a separate schedule or appendix, although clearly they should remain as intrinsic constituents of the contract.

The charges may range from a global fixed price for the whole contract, through daily rates and direct costs, to intricate formulae for individual calculations. Components of the charges – such as staff or contractors' costs, data volumes and equipment rental – may be separately identified and itemized.

Allowance should be made for adjusting the charges during the life of the contract, to accommodate variations to the services or to enable the supplier to cover its own rising costs. The customer may require an opportunity to renegotiate if economies are anticipated over time due to the supplier's efficiency or the introduction of more effective technological applications, or where the contract is for a lengthy fixed term.

Commercial evaluation

The customer's internal IT department costs are often treated as an overhead. Costs associated with IT may include those for the resources: the personnel and the management of the staff; office accommodation; computer hardware and networks; software licences; project development and implementation; and the recurring costs of maintenance and support.

In evaluating outsourcing charges, the customer should ideally be making direct comparisons with its own budget. The projected costs of outsourcing can be compared over the years of the proposed contract term with the projected costs of retaining the service in-house. This must be done realistically, to take account of any changes which may arise from falling technology costs as well as from requirements for new developments and more sophisticated systems. In practice, many customers do not have enough information to enable them to make an informed estimate of any potential savings.

In whatever way the charges are assessed, a familiar argument is that an individual customer is not going to be able to make the sorts of saving that one supplier acting for a number of customers can effect through economies of scale. The optimistic supplier's argument is that there are bound to be savings in all areas – hardware, software licences, site costs, staff and their expertise, help desk, back up and recovery and other security matters. Some suppliers are undoubtedly going to be more cost-effective than the customer's previous internally organized management services department, either generally in providing information systems or running IT operations or specifically in providing a particular service. One central help desk for a particular system platform may service end users from a number of different customer companies. The same hardware may be used efficiently for a range of customers, and there may therefore be gains as a result of price reduction through performance-related technology improvements. The supplier may have negotiated a single licence with standard software suppliers. A number of customers' requirements may be able to be covered by a small number of technically experienced staff. The supplier's services may be able to be standardized thereby achieving savings in overheads. The supplier may be in a position to cut costs safely in ways which were politically unacceptable for an in-house service to effect.

The supplier will claim business experience in its customers' industries and that it is continuously keeping up-to-date technologically. This will be argued to be for the benefit of its customers.

To some extent, cost savings depend on the nature of the outsourcing. Economies of scale are more easily demonstrable on stable mainframe and operations outsourcing, but less obvious on systems development.

The converse argument is that any such economies can also be achieved by an efficient in-house department which does not have substantial promotional costs and which does not have to make a profit in its operation. Indirectly, the supplier's charges have to allow for new activities arising from the management of an external function – that is, management reviews of performance, audits and control of variations.

A large customer organization whose operations are extensive, whose name is well known and which has a number of subsidiary or associated companies, may have negotiated its own discounts for the supply of technology or licence fees which it may be reluctant to forego for an outsourcing arrangement. Although licence transfer fees can be costly, the customer may gain little benefit from the supplier having its own site licence.

If the outsourcing costs appear to be favourable, the customer may have to assess whether there are ways in which it could itself make equivalent savings in-house over a period of time. Where the outsourcing costs do not seem to be attractive, other factors may be brought into the equation. In deciding whether the supplier can provide the services more cheaply than the current in-house facility or whether the in-house department is more cost-effective, the implications of what the suppliers are offering must be reviewed.

Capital or revenue?

The customer's financial motives may go further than a cost-cutting rationale or seeking predictability of costs. In some cases, outsourcing will enable capital to be removed from a company's balance sheet with the immediate strategic advantage of converting a fixed cost capital basis for IT activities to the variable costs of revenue-based IT services. The customer is therefore transforming fixed data processing assets into variable costs and will no longer have to find the capital to finance new technology or to make large-scale future investment in IT.

When the supplier acquires equipment and staff from the customer, this may release capital and other financial resources. The main IT costs are for staff, and the most obvious way for the customer to make savings will be through the transfer of its IT staff to the supplier. This will reduce at one fell swoop the customer's overall IT costs and aid its ongoing training and recruitment budget. The supplier may be able to make efficient use of the staff it acquires by using them for its services for the customer or elsewhere within its organization. The employment and career path of the transferred personnel will no longer be determined by the customer's IT requirements.

The customer may purchase a computer for cash or obtain it on a financial lease. In this latter case, a liability in respect of that lease will be created on the balance sheet for the future cash requirements associated with the lease. Either way, the effect is to increase the gearing – that is, the ratio of the amount of the company's capital in the form of debt to the amount in the form of shareholders' equity. Given that the computer – and linked equipment – is depreciating (otherwise the advantage gained will be only short-term), it can be sold to the supplier as part of the outsourcing arrangements, and the debt represented by it on the balance sheet will be removed. This will assist in reducing the customer's gearing. Money tied up on the balance sheet on non-financial assets, such as cars, property and computers, can be more valuable if released for the organization's core activities. It will also be a factor in the outsourcing evaluation by a company with too much debt.

As part of the overall balancing of the transaction, the supplier may make an up-front cash payment to the customer by purchasing assets – equipment, land and buildings, and staff resources. This may be by means of a cash transaction or a loan

at a favourable rate, thereby generating more financial flexibility for the customer's corporate activities at the initial stage
of outsourcing, by converting future capital expenditure on IT
into regular service charges without the burden of their fixed
overheads. This is a restricted and short-term view of the
potential benefits of outsourcing, but nevertheless may be of
immense practical immediate benefit to certain customer organizations in certain straitened situations.

For a few customers in serious short-term financial difficulties, the reasons for outsourcing may even be entirely financial,
in terms of restructuring their balance sheet and improving
their cash flow. The supplier may creatively put together an
attractive deal, postponing payments for services, injecting cash
into the enterprise and showing that tax gains may be realiz-
able. Any other benefits in terms of efficiency, cheaper or
improved services will be side-effects. In this context, outsourcing can be construed merely as an imperative cost-cutting
exercise. Such customers should consider the ultimate value of
short-term financial gains and what is to happen when the
contract comes to an end. On its part, the supplier must
certainly consider whether such a contractual relationship
would be genuinely attractive.

Associated costs

The customer's budget for outsourcing IT must always include
those costs which will be incurred in the preparation for
outsourcing, which can be surprisingly high. It was reported[1]
that expenditure by Customs and Excise totalled £2 million
when it carried out its market test for computer services and
professional consultancy services for a contract estimated at
£100 millions' worth of IT business. This included the costs of
hiring consultants, the preparation work and bid evaluation. In
this case, the contract was eventually awarded to the in-house
team.

The direct costs payable by the customer will include external
professional fees such as those for outsourcing consultants and

specialist legal advice, including drafting and negotiating the relevant contracts. There will also be internal management time and effort involved, from selecting the supplier through negotiating the commercial considerations to the administration and execution of the contract.

Additional costs will be incurred in communicating with potential suppliers, by open advertisements in the public sector or by means of direct contacts. The invitation to tender or other means of conveying information and asking for proposals must be prepared and distributed. The resulting tenderers' proposals must be evaluated, and the eventual selection made. There will be direct costs associated with transferring assets and resources and in obtaining the necessary rights for the use of the licensed software by the supplier, whether by assignment or otherwise. Indirect costs of time will be involved in agreeing service levels and effort expended in keeping end users informed and contented.

In budgeting for the operation of the contract, unanticipated costs in the service provision should always be allowed for in addition to the charges estimated for the services. There will also be the costs of liaison management, contract management, audit and other residual costs for those functions retained in-house.

'In virtually every supplier-written contract we studied, we uncovered hidden costs, some adding up to hundreds of thousands – even millions – of dollars'.[2] Hopefully, this pessimistic warning should not be relevant for the customer following the advice given in this book, since a customized contract to meet individual requirements will be drawn up.

The supplier's perspective

A supplier carries out outsourcing with a view to making a profit, and it is in its customers' interests that it should do so. A supplier operating on tight margins will not be able to make improvements or innovate in its service provision.

The supplier will get no value out of a contract taken on purely because it has made the cheapest bid competitively without considering its profitability requirements. In order to do this, various associated indirect factors must be taken into account in calculating the contract price.

Indirectly there will be the costs of the supplier's unsuccessful bids for outsourcing contracts. One contract gained from every six attempts is likely to be a good rate. One out of ten is probably more typical. General sales and marketing promotional expenses should not be underestimated. Long-term cash flow has to be considered. At the outset of an outsourcing relationship, the supplier will have made a significant investment in taking over the installation, moving workloads to another machine, perhaps setting up at another site and taking on the customer's staff. It may have to look long-term at making the greater part of its profit in later years by achieving operating efficiency and price performance in its service provision.

Suppliers do not appear to be differentiated primarily on charges, although significant differences do arise in individual responses to an invitation to tender. Within a reasonable range of different charges, the customer's final selection of a supplier tends to be influenced by other characteristics of the proposals and presentations.

Invitation to tender

The invitation to tender may be highly specific in seeking a fixed charging structure over the term of the contract, or it may request innovative costing proposals, seeking flexibility in ways of reducing costs and adding value. Inflation, productivity and efficiency improvements should be addressed. Joint ventures are discussed in Chapter 3. In the invitation to tender, the customer may ask for proposals from suppliers for creating joint ventures.

Tenderers should be asked to make it clear what is being excluded from their proposals and what assumptions they are making, to ensure that comparisons are being made on a fair basis. For example, they may be assuming a given level of inflation over the contract term. They may anticipate that licence fees will be separately negotiated. Their charges may be based on the customer accepting all the services from a single supplier rather than splitting the services up among a number of them. Certain third-party expenses may be included in the costs or may be separate. If the service costs are split into distinct areas of services, the customer's evaluation of the bids will be made easier. The bids should include details of additional charges, such as payments to third parties and how transferred assets will be paid for.

Where the main costs are to be fixed, development may also be treated as part of the core service up to a fixed number of hours or days, and then at a daily resource rate outside the core service.

Charging bases

The services may be provided at a fixed price or at a rate based on time, activity or volumes, and may extend to cost plus profit element for the supplier, open-book accounting or reward-sharing. There may be a combination of different charging methods covering different parts of the services. The trends today are towards open-book accounting and shared risk/ rewards.

On start-up, the customer may make an initial payment to the supplier for the transfer of its services. Conversely, the supplier may sometimes pay the customer for the acquisition of hardware assets, or on the transfer of staff by the customer.

The supplier's service charges will comprise a number of elements: regular payments for the services; some incidentals; and also direct costs. Recurring charges will be for the delivery of services, and it is up to the supplier how the resources should be managed in order to make a profit from the charges levied. There may be an agreed aim that resources should be gradually reduced over the contract term to achieve greater efficiencies and lower fixed costs. The charges may be expressed as unit costs or broken down in a number of ways according to various formulae or related to performance parameters, such as operating hours or workloads.

The customer will need to recognize that there will be a trade-off between costs and service. Suppliers will implement cost control measures to save costs. They may have loss-leading first-year contracts which rise in cost in subsequent years or where the fixed price does not cover services which are bound to be needed at added prices. Sometimes users become more selective in justifying their requirements when the relation between payment and service provision becomes apparent. It may happen that a lower level of services than those expected when the services were provided in-house will become acceptable to end users, and that changes will cost more to implement.

It is not uncommon to have a system allowing rebates to the service charges, by service credits or by liquidated damages payable for failure to reach service levels. This is discussed in Chapter 5.

Fixed price

A fixed price provided by an outsourcing supplier will seem an attractive prospect to a Board whose members are unsympathetic to the difficulties of predicting IT costs, yet who are aware that such costs always seem to be increasing.

In its simplest form, this is a price agreed between the supplier and the customer for the term of the contract. It may be expressed as an annual charge for each of the years of the contract's life.

For this kind of pricing arrangement, the contract should be short-term or one in which the deliverables and volumes can be accurately predicted and controlled. It is suitable where the requirements are well defined and where no changes are envisaged. It might be used when an obsolescent system likely to be of a short-term duration is being handed over for outsourcing until its replacement becomes fully operational, or for systems which are self-contained or which have very limited interaction with other systems.

The contract may recognize the specific circumstances in which the fixed price will be increased as a result of changed or increased activities and volumes, or the introduction of new technology.

The risk for the supplier is that the fixed price will not cover all the elements involved in the services. The supplier may adjust its service delivery to retain its profit margin if the costs of providing the service increase because of factors outside its control. The risks for the customer are therefore that the levels of services deteriorate and that variations will cost more to implement. This is allied to the view that 'there is no such thing as a fixed price contract', because there will always be unforeseen circumstances. Higher prices may then apply to amendments which are subsequently settled on a time and materials basis.

In practice with a fixed price contract, there is most likely to be a basic banded fixed price or a minimum charge, together with a rate which changes, based on agreed procedures and according to the varying number of users, employees or accounts.

Time and materials

In this arrangement, payment is by unit pricing according to actual usage. The usage might be of various kinds of resources, ranging from computer time to human resources.

Connect time to the computer is one form of rate that can be measured easily: for example, by machine time per second; connect time per hour; storage costs in terms of media; length of time of storage; and volumes.

The normal payment method for development and programming work would be at an hourly or daily resource rate according to seniority and experience, dependent on time spent.

The risk is that the charging method will be perceived to be open-ended. This risk can be contained by limits specified in the contract, such as estimated ceilings or early warnings by the supplier of increases to the estimated costs, so that the customer has a choice, at least in principle, of whether to accept the higher charges or whether to prioritize or to forego some requirements. In practice, the choice may not be entirely open if the customer is dependent on the services.

Sharing profits or savings

Here, the supplier must disclose to the customer information about the composition of the costs of running the services and its profits earned in providing the services, through 'open-book' procedures.

The charges will then consist of the costs together with a management fee on top. Alternatively, the supplier may take an agreed percentage as profit. If the profits turn out to be greater than expected, the differences will be split between supplier and customer.

Open-book charges are appropriate for variable costs. One example where open-book charges are used, with or without management fees, is for staff costs, particularly for contract staff used on development work. Another is for capacity usage.

Alternatively, a budget for some or all of the costs may be agreed between the supplier and the customer at the start of each year, and savings made beyond that shared equally or on some other basis. For example, incentives may be agreed in the contract by creating formulae for establishing when reductions in staff costs or service delivery are achieved so that, where ongoing savings are realized, they are allocated proportionately as agreed.

Agreed target costs can be established, to be paid to the supplier by the customer. The actual costs will be ascertained through audit. If the actual costs exceed the target costs, so that the savings from the contract for the customer are less than anticipated, the supplier will also take a loss, the shortfall being shared between the parties in the agreed proportions. If the actual costs are less than the target costs, the gain will be shared. The supplier will always be paid the target costs. The contract will detail the potential costs overrun or gain which the customer and supplier agree.

These charging methods act as an incentive for the supplier and will benefit both parties where the services are amenable to improvement.

Ancillary expenses and charges

Some third-party charges may be payable by the customer, directly to the third party or via the supplier, such as contractors' charges, third-party licence charges, hardware maintenance and software support. Other costs which arise from time to time, such as training courses, may also be charged for additionally and directly.

The contract should define what expenses may be claimed, and what are excluded, as well as when agreement in advance is required before expenses may be claimed. Receipts for actual expenditure may also be required. Should travel by the supplier's staff to the customer's sites be allowable as expenses? When is hotel accommodation permissible? Would attendance at meetings called by the customer over and above the contractual review procedures attract expenses for the supplier's senior staff? What about charges for time spent in responding to third-party auditors' questions?

Variations to the charges

The review of charges is important. In all but the simplest short-term fixed price contract with no scope for extension, procedures and parameters for varying the charges should be stated. A supplier has to keep pace with rates of inflation and, in particular, with salary increases in the IT industry. It must have the right to increase its charges at some point, unless its quote has been purely on the basis of a fixed price or rate for a limited time.

However, some contractual control should be exercised by the customer over rates of increases which are acceptable, so that the supplier does not have unfettered power to control its charges.

There should be a set period from the commencement of the contract during which the charges will not be increased. Thereafter, increases should be allowed only at limited intervals, such as not more frequently than at 12-month intervals, and confined to a reasonable level. This may be done by linking increases to some index. The Retail Prices Index is often used, to account for inflation. Since staff salaries are such a significant part of the outsourcing provider's budget, a mutually agreed computer salaries index may be more relevant. The NCC carries out annual surveys of salary and staff issues in computing across job categories and industry sectors. The Employment Index for computer staff is published annually by Computer Economics. Salary Survey Publications carries out a quarterly survey, including salaries, by analysing recruitment advertising in the trade press and national and provincial daily press. The addresses of these organizations are set out in Chapter 15.

While limiting increases to the charges, it is to be anticipated that some running costs should decrease over the term of the contract. The unit costs of IT drop exponentially over time. Old legacy systems can be replaced with lower-cost hardware and software packages. If customers do not appreciate this, they will be paying the same fees over the contract term and failing to gain from potential savings.

Any variation to the services may carry cost implications. The change control procedure is described in Chapter 11, and any increased charges as a result of the variation must be agreed in advance of proceeding with the change.

Payment methods

How the supplier is to be paid will affect its cash flow and will therefore indirectly affect its charges. The recurring payments for service provision may be made at monthly or quarterly intervals, or by instalments, and in advance or in arrears. There may need to be end-of-year reconciliations where payments were made on the basis of estimates. Expenses and non-recurring agreed charges are typically paid for in arrears, monthly or quarterly.

VAT will be payable in addition to the charges, and there should be a statement in the contract to this effect.

It is reasonable for the supplier to minimize its risk of non-payment or late payment by reserving the right to charge interest in the event of late payment. The rate of interest must be one normally found commercially for it to be contractually enforceable. It is normally stated as being a small percentage above the bank rate of one of the clearing banks, accruing on a daily basis. The supplier may choose not to enforce the payment of interest – for example, if the relationship is generally satisfactory and late payment by the customer has occurred inadvertently only on one occasion.

The supplier may also wish to include a provision for suspension or termination of the service in the event of non-payment. The customer may negotiate for this to follow a formal notice giving a number of days' grace, in case the non-payment is merely due to an administrative error. Services important to running the business should not be suspended without warning. However, suspension of service may be a reasonable lever for the supplier whose payments are consistently delayed.

If a dispute arises, the customer may seek to suspend payments. If negotiations to resolve the dispute are in progress, there can be a provision in the contract for the payments relating to the matter in dispute to be made to an interest-bearing deposit account in the parties' joint names. Following resolution of the dispute the sum can be paid out to the parties as agreed by the settlement, and interest allocated pro rata according to the distribution of the principal sum.

Monitoring charges

To discover whether benefits which it was assumed would be achieved following the move to outsourcing are in fact being realized, the customer should monitor the charges as well as the service levels, in order to obtain a true picture of the value of the outsourcing services over the life of the contract.

This monitoring may take place at a number of levels. The ongoing costs should be compared from time to time with the costs predicted at the outset by the supplier and as estimated by the customer. It may be salutary to recall the in-house budget plans, had outsourcing not proceeded.

It may be possible to benchmark services against similar services provided to organizations which are equivalent to the customer's in terms of size and complexity, if any can be found. Where it is difficult to agree on comparable organizations overall, it may be possible to break down the services and related charges into discrete categories for individual comparisons to be made. This will not be entirely satisfactory, as various allowances will have to be built into the assessments.

Various commercial performance benchmark indices are available, such as categories of unit costs. There are various market surveys, such as the Computer Economics staff costs surveys. Market surveys may also be commissioned and paid for by the customer or jointly by the parties for those services whose costs are being measured but for which there are no criteria.

The results of the monitoring should be tabled occasionally for discussion at a review meeting. If an objective analysis and comparison can be made to establish the value being obtained from outsourcing, this will provide an informed basis for ascertaining whether the outsourcing is a qualified success or unmitigated failure. It should be agreed in the contract that, where there are shortcomings, plans should be drawn up and agreed within a specified time for the purpose of improving the services and adjusting the charges.

Clauses on charges and costings should be negotiated by the customer with the objective of confirming value for money throughout the period of the contract.

Notes

1   *Computer Weekly*, 29 February 1996.
2   Mary C. Lacity, Leslie P. Willcocks & David F. Feeny, 'IT Outsourcing: Maximise Flexibility and Control', *Harvard Business Review*, May-June 1995.

10 Management liaison and review

Once the outsourcing contract has come into effect, the management of the continuing relationship between supplier and customer is of enormous importance. The mechanisms for the liaison between customer and supplier should be discussed when the contract is being negotiated. A clear understanding of the division of functions and roles between them is essential and should be set out formally and in detail in the contract. This is all part of the balance of cooperation and control.

It is easy to underestimate the customer management responsibilities that will continue to exist under an IT outsourcing arrangement. Control is a fundamental part of a customer's ability to retain leverage over the supplier whose own objectives include making a profit. It is not enough for the customer only to note, at the time of paying the invoices, that the services continue in general to be provided. It is not adequate merely to check that the bills relate approximately to the volumes and response times specified as the service levels. The outsourcing must be coherently managed by the customer in order to be effective. Management should be entrusted to one or more persons with sufficient calibre and professional competence at least equivalent to the supplier's.

For other bought-in services, overall supervision is normal. Externally provided services, such as marketing campaigns, transport organization and legal requirements, will be carried out with some involvement and decision-making on the part of the client organization's director or line manager responsible, or by a management team especially brought together for the purpose. However, these other services may be supplied as individual transactions, or may be for a single function or may last for a matter of weeks or months and be easier to discard if performance is erratic or otherwise ineffective. Outsourcing services are continuous, more pervasive and will last longer. It is therefore crucial for the customer to be aware of how they are being carried out, and to ensure that they continue to meet the customer's requirements, even in changing circumstances.

Customer management function

For outsourcing services, the essential customer management function will cover responsibility for assessing current performance, prioritizing future requirements and controlling variations. This sets in the customer's business context the services which are being provided, to the agreed standards, for the price being paid. Without this management capability, a customer will have no means of knowing if the charges are reasonable or whether the service levels are being satisfactorily maintained.

In its control and planning, the customer will therefore take a range of considerations into account. The demands of end users and the existing relationship with them, successful coordination of the different systems, its business policy and future requirements and its cultural style have all to be integrated.

It follows that division of the responsibilities should entail the supplier managing the services themselves and the control of their delivery day-to-day, while the customer must manage how the services will fit in with the strategic direction of its business, with formal review points. The customer must retain ultimate responsibility both for making its business decisions and its IT strategy. It may be guided in this by listening to advice or strong recommendations from the outsourcing supplier or from third-party consultants. Within this basic division, the extent of control retained by the customer should be a matter for negotiation.

For example, in one telecommunications outsourcing of corporate wide area voice and data networks, the supplier's extensive commitments covered infrastructure management, migration and a high level of user project management. The customer's in-house core team retained the overall architecture and consequently took charge of controlling strategy, standards and security. However, the supplier was encouraged to contribute to these areas, especially in seeking new network capabilities and services.

In another outsourcing arrangement, by a manufacturer of its commercial IT operations, together with some development work, hardware maintenance and network management for its factories, it was the manufacturer's in-house team which established policies and procedures, dealt with the management of the contract and service-level agreement, and with the interface between end users and suppliers.

If the customer has the resources to do so, it may wish to take a more interventionist approach. Some companies may have their reasons for retaining control over the final selection of replacement hardware and software. Are all third-party payments to be made directly by the supplier?

Depending on the nature of the outsourcing, the supplier may require the customer to accept responsibility for the preparation and accuracy of its own data and notification of any special features and delivery required to an agreed timescale so that, if the outputs are not met in time or satisfactorily as a result of inadequate data, the supplier will not be liable.

Internal or external customer appointment

The existing IT management function will therefore change once the outsourcing process starts, as different skills will be required for the new liaison management role. The customer will no longer have extensive staff management demands. General management abilities and financial understanding are desirable, as is an awareness of the technical issues, to identify technological innovations brought to the marketplace, to keep up with changes in demand from users, and to assess whether technical failures are being properly resolved. Negotiating skills will be necessary, whether for handling complaints from end users or for discussions with the supplier, in order to be able to solve any problems within the contractual framework to the satisfaction of everyone concerned, while keeping the relationships amicable and professional. The customer will therefore need to draw on wider skills than may previously have been used, including financial and technical expertise, common sense and judgement, team building and team bonding, in order to derive the best out of the outsourcing experience.

In addition to the general management of the outsourcing function, the customer will be well advised to retain, or acquire, some in-house technical capability in order to understand the operation of the contracted services. One statement of the ideal is: 'Retain just enough in-house expertise to check up on supplier performance, keep up with technical issues and devise the next strategy.'[1]

This is not to say that it will inevitably be the same members of the customer's existing staff who were formerly charged with management functions who will be tasked with the liaison management, although this will frequently be the case. It may be that there is no single person employed by the customer who is suitable for the new role. It may be necessary for new appointments to be made – of a liaison services manager or team from outside – or for consultancy expertise to be bought in for managing the liaison process. The customer should still allocate an IT budget to allow for an in-house function, however much reduced in amount, and this factor should be taken into account in the costing equations.

For the management and liaison process to be effective, there should be a direct reporting channel at the customer's Board level (or its equivalent where the organizational structure is not a corporate one), whether the liaison services role is an internal or an external service function in the customer organization.

Project representatives

In any event, representatives at senior level should be appointed by each party. They will each play a key part in the liaison process. The responsibilities of each will differ, but both should have sufficient authority to be able to act and take decisions on behalf of their respective organizations, and to be able to give or receive information required by the other. Each representative needs to be more than a liaison officer without any real power to influence the course of events, particularly when decisions may need to be made (and sometimes made quickly) concerning services performance, variation or additions, to keep the arrangement on course or to overcome deviations.

The individual roles of the representatives will influence the titles which they are to be given. Are they to be regarded as account managers, project managers or contract managers? It is recommended for convenience that the customer representative should have a different title from the supplier representative. They will have different functions and it will be easier to draft the contract and to understand it from the different perspectives and roles of the representatives.

For a large outsourcing project a steering team for either or both parties may be necessary, with responsibilities shared among the members.

Considerable difficulties would arise if the supplier and customer representatives were unable to work together. For a major outsourcing, the customer may reasonably expect to have some say in the appointment of the supplier's representative, or even to have designated representatives, agreed by the customer or by both parties, named in a schedule to the contract. Curriculum vitae may be required on the appointment or replacement of individuals. If this is agreed, some reasonable parameters need to be set, so that there is no arbitrary exclusion. There may have to be procedures agreed in the selection of a replacement, and time allowed for the process.

One particular individual may be crucial to the customer's selection of a supplier. For example, in a small supplier company the managing director may be taking a keen personal interest in the success of the outsourcing. That person may be named as key to the contract but, in the interests of both parties, the extent of that indispensability needs to be agreed, and the contract must be able to survive any individual move or transfer.

Consideration should be given to channelling all communications concerning service performance through the nominated representatives. There is certainly a need to channel day-to-day operational liaison so as to prevent a possible cacophony of conflicting voices and also to avoid obstructing necessary communications. In practice, this would require some care. If it is decided that this would be a desirable method of working, deputies should also be nominated so that there is always a decision-maker available.

Project liaison description

The description of the project liaison role will include a number of activities for each party, some of which are listed below. Some may be specified as contractual requirements, but they will not all be appropriate for both the supplier's and the customer's representatives, and it would not normally be essential to make the list a lengthy one. It may be wise not to be too dogmatic.

- **Services and monitoring**
  - assessing contract performance, by monitoring the service against the contract and against the service levels agreed
  - resolving inadequacies in existing services
  - monitoring security and contingency procedures

- reviewing the accuracy of documentation, especially after variations to the services have been introduced
- monitoring change control procedures
- providing regular statistics and reports
- interpreting and reviewing the reports and statistics
- audit rights.
- **Contract**
  - keeping the contract, schedules and appendices and service-level agreements up-to-date
  - keeping staff informed as necessary of the contractual commitments – for example, concerning confidentiality, agreed turnround times, payment schedules.
- **Communication**
  - managing demand for the services
  - communicating with end users, getting feedback on a formal basis and ensuring that their needs are addressed within the contract constraints
  - identifying and addressing training needs of staff – customer's, supplier's, end users'
  - attending, organizing, minuting and running the liaison meetings
  - cooperating with the other party's representative.
- **Planning**
  - articulating variations and identifying possible or necessary new services
  - long-term strategy
  - contract renegotiation.

The representatives should be able to coordinate the technical and financial knowledge with those staff who hold key responsibilities in these areas.

Relationship with end users

If end users are involved in the outsourcing, they must have a channel for communicating their requirements. If there are many end users or if there are different kinds of end users, some coordination will be necessary. This may be effected through the customer representative or it may be appropriate for the end users to interact directly with the supplier. The choice of communication route will be influenced by: how end user variations are to be introduced; how the charges made by the supplier relate to the usage by end users; and the relationship of the customer management with its end users.

In providing the services, the supplier may be close to the end users and in a position to recommend attractive new solutions which will require further expenditure by the customer. This needs to be controlled by means of a designated procedure for channelling end user requests for more resources or updated technology via the customer's representative.

Once the contract is in effect, end users will be alert in critically noticing any differences in the service provision from what they were previously receiving. The tasks of the customer's outsourcing manager should include regular liaison with end users, in order to learn promptly of any operational problems or new ideas, so that action may be taken wherever possible to remedy or enhance the service provision.

Cooperation and goodwill are essential in outsourcing as in computing arrangements generally, but this need not be at the expense of objective ongoing analysis and assessment which will be critical to long-term success. This assessment can be effected by means of formal meetings and review procedures for assessing the reports and the service-level statistics of performance and results. Each party should draw up its own internal procedures to reflect its own responsibilities of what is agreed in the contract.

Reports and statistics

The supplier's principal responsibility is to carry out the services as stipulated in the contract, and there should be willingness to demonstrate this in practice to the customer. To assist in this, regular reports and statistics will be a contractual requirement.

The supplier will be expected to produce performance reports to show compliance with service levels, exception reports, trend analyses and charts, and various other reports and statistics, monthly or quarterly. Nevertheless, it must be remembered that the supplier's effort in producing the paperwork to report and substantiate the provision of the services will be reflected in the overall costs of the services. It is therefore worth spending time when the contract is being negotiated in agreeing what methods will be the most useful for assessing the effectiveness of the services provision.

The manner of presenting the performance reports should be agreed, but not necessarily crystallized as part of the contract terms. If the reports are found to be useful in practice, better ways of making them efficient references may be requested by the customer.

It should be stipulated when the reports are to be made available, particularly so as to allow time for perusal in advance of any meetings where they are to be the subject of discussion.

Meetings and reviews

The outsourcing customer needs a structured method of monitoring and reviewing the services. There is nothing new about this. In Barbara Tuchman's account of the calamitous fourteenth century,[2] she describes the review or *montre* for knights and squires in war service to their ruler. In those days armies had little structure with no proper hierarchy of command. There were standard rates of pay for nobles according to status, and the King had to ensure that he was getting the level of quality for which he was paying. Generally, the review would be carried out monthly by officials on the lookout for valets being substituted for their masters, and vigilant to detect whether healthy horses presented for their approval would be replaced by old nags for battle.

A framework of formal meetings and reviews, and the ways in which they will operate, should be set out in the contract.

Depending on the complexity of the outsourcing, there may be several review levels. For example, in Pilkington's contract with EDS for management of its head office applications, three types of meetings were set up:

- a business management meeting to monitor the contract
- an operational review meeting to plan and monitor services
- functional steering groups established to progress information systems plans.

This means that decisions need to be taken on what different kinds of review points should be established, for what functions. How often should the meetings take place? How prescriptive should their format be? How far should their administrative procedures be elaborated as a basis for successful checks and balances over the life of the contract?

At a minimum the appointed representatives of each party, together with other members of the teams involved, should meet regularly – perhaps monthly as a good starting-point, possibly more frequently at the outset. This should not inhibit normal day-to-day informal discussion of progress by the representatives between the meetings.

The primary focus of these meetings will be on the review of the performance of service levels. Reports and statistics will be prepared as part of the overall review process for noting or for discussion. The reports to be prepared by the supplier should be listed, together with a stipulation of how far in advance of the meeting they should be available and whether they are to be produced for every meeting or from time to time. At best, the meetings and reports will confirm that all is working as anticipated. If service levels are related to payment, this will be material to justify submission of the supplier's invoices.

Adverse trends can be identified and appropriate action initiated. In this way the meetings can act as an early warning system and, ideally, as a means of foreseeing problems to obviate them. Of course, the meeting will also be the forum for creating positive solutions to problems which have already arisen.

At these meetings, variations to the services may be proposed and negotiated. Either party may suggest ways of enhancing, adding value to, increasing or decreasing the scope of the services.

When there are no alarms, all is apparently running smoothly, and it becomes difficult to find mutually agreeable dates for the meetings, they should still continue to be held at the agreed intervals. They should remain the focal point for raising any issues or discussing exceptions. In their absence, a false sense of security may easily be engendered. Unanticipated problems may gradually emerge or unresolved tensions or resentment may build up, which a short airing would have resolved.

The meetings should reinforce the spirit of cooperation between the representatives and therefore collaborative effort between the supplier and customer's staff as a whole. Nevertheless, both representatives must remember that they hold their positions on behalf of their respective organizations and that their interests are therefore not identical. Within the scope of the contract it cannot be assumed that all will be bound to be well in the best of all possible worlds.

Responsibility should be allocated for drawing up the agenda. It may include:

- notes of the previous meeting and matters arising
- review and discussion of service performance against service level agreements
- specific problems
- administrative issues
- proposed changes, requests for enhancements, modifications, new services or products
- any other business.

There is a strong argument in favour of the customer's representative chairing the meeting, as part of its fundamental control of outsourcing strategy.

One party should be in charge of preparing and distributing notes from the meeting, although they should be agreed by both parties. These notes should consist of records of what was agreed and commitments to be undertaken as actions arising from the meeting. If the meeting notes are to be used actively as working documents, it can sometimes be helpful to summarize briefly the reasons for the decisions taken. Confessionals are to be avoided, however. If problems do arise, it is not helpful to have a complete account of the candid exchange of views which may have occurred at the meeting. It is not unknown for such minutes to become an embarrassing permanent record of senior members of staff bewailing the poor quality of their own products, services or lack of control.

At the next level up from the standard progress meetings, strategic reviews will be required less regularly – quarterly, six-monthly or annually. The emphasis will be away from the practicalities of normal monitoring and administrative pro-cesses, the objective being to consider whether any new business directions will affect the scope and provision of the services and any ways in which the services can be streamlined, adapted and improved to give better value. It will be useful to note whether decisions are being taken at the right level and whether senior management is being involved too often or too little. Are problems normally being sorted out satisfactorily with minimal paperwork but with a record of what was agreed? These reviews will typically be conducted at Board or senior management level for each party – that is, officials who are at some remove from any role – although the senior outsourcing representatives will also participate.

For reference purposes, the formats for the meetings and strategic reviews, listing the personnel taking part and the procedures to be followed, should be recorded in a document which can be physically accessed independently of the contract, perhaps in the form of a schedule.

The control exercised by the customer through meetings and reviews may be tighter at the start of the relationship, at a time when the informal mechanisms are not yet established, when it may not be clear whether the service levels will all be realistic, when there may be apprehension on the part of the customer and when the supplier may not yet have become familiar with the customer's systems. However, if the regulatory mechanisms should loosen, this should be as a result of a deliberate decision by the customer, not on account of indolence.

Escalation procedures

When representatives are appointed, responsibilities allocated and procedures established, problems will be minimized, but this provides no guarantee that they will be avoided altogether. Wherever complicated affairs are being managed, differences can normally be expected to emerge occasionally between the supplier and customer. It is nevertheless disheartening when conflicts do arise, whether these are through perceived inadequacies in communication or in carrying out the service activities or because of different perceptions, or because of other apparent shortcomings.

Where different groups of people are working together over a period of time, problems can emerge from trivial causes. Experienced managers should be able to handle many potential confrontations, where areas of responsibilities, chains of command and reporting structures have been put in place. For example, consultants from companies which would have liked to win the outsourcing work but which failed in their overall bids, may still be supplying specialist services to the customer in individual areas and be working alongside the supplier's staff. A contractual commitment should be given by the supplier that it will cooperate with any third-party contractors providing services to the customer. The third-party contractors' contracts should likewise contain an obligation of co-operation.

The meetings which have been set up will be the normal forum at which complaints may be raised and resulting courses of action proposed. Yet there will be occasions when the normal channels for communication and reporting will not work satisfactorily. To allow for this, an escalation procedure should be set out in the contract. At times of controversy, these known channels for attempting to resolve disagreements can be adopted sooner rather than later, with the aim of clearing the problem out of the way and returning to the primary purpose of running the contract.

Unresolved problems will be referred up to senior decision-makers not immediately involved. They will have a perspective distanced from the daily involvement in the services, which can often make solutions to problems easier to reach.

The escalation procedure should define the point at which the next level of authority will be invoked. This may be triggered within a specified timespan – days or even hours according to the seriousness of the predicament – or through the general meetings and strategic reviews in the first instance. A number of tiers may be agreed, up to Board level referral or its equivalent for both organizations, with final appeal to an expert or arbitrator. Methods of formal dispute resolution for breach of contract if the escalation procedures do not succeed are discussed in Chapter 14.

The overriding object is to sort out any problem as soon as possible in order to carry on with the outsourcing process and preferably to keep a positive working relationship.

Independent audit

The contract should allow for periodic audits to be carried out. An 'audit' used simply to be a financial audit to check that all sums were accounted for and that no fraud was taking place. Now the term is more widely used for various reviews or checks and even for collecting and collating information. For monitoring and review of the outsourcing, both internal and external audit procedures may be called for.

Those organizations which are accredited with ISO 9000 will already be familiar with internal and external audits to demonstrate continuing compliance with formal procedures.

It may be that the customer organization will already employ internal auditors for reviewing its systems. The primary UK professional body for internal auditors is the Institute of Internal Auditors; auditors belonging to this Institute have a professional qualification achieved by examination, following a two-year course and evidence of practical experience. The Institute's syllabus covers principles and practice of management theory, accounting, control, finance, business analysis and systems auditing. Thus they are well placed for examination of business and computing systems as well as accounts.

However, the internal auditors may have other qualifications or have been appointed by virtue of experience gained within the organization through familiarity with its business practices or elsewhere.

For an external review of the outsourcing processes, an independent auditor on behalf of the customer must be acceptable to the outsourcing provider. For example, chartered accountants are recognized under the Companies Acts as qualified to be auditors by virtue of their training. Chartered information system engineers or practitioners will also have the competence to undertake external audits. The external auditor will provide a professional opinion, reporting on the findings of compliance with the statistics produced in respect of service levels and performance standards and, where relevant, their relation to the charges imposed.

The details of control of the outsourcing by the deployment of representatives, meeting schedules and formalities, statistics and reports required should therefore be set out in the contract, the balance of control lying with the customer which must retain at a senior level the responsibility for strategy and planning focus. It is the customer's job to ensure that the IT continues to meet the needs of the business, to promote IT regularly in its business and to maintain the investment – allowing for changes in technology. It cannot discard its evaluation and decision-making capability. It must still take decisions about business development and systems integration. It must be seen to be managing the contract.

Notes

1   Richard Brett, Group Director of the CAA, writing in the *MBA Newsletter*, July 1995.
2   Barbara W. Tuchman (1978), *A Distant Mirror*, London: Macmillan.

11 Allowing for change

Change is integral to the computer industry. For any decision taken on which hardware, software or system to buy, or about which skills to send employees on training courses to acquire, six months later there will be more choice with different, more versatile and cheaper new offerings in the market. Like computer professionals, a number of Alan Coren's university contemporaries in the Foreign Office found themselves in this state which he described as 'permanent dynamic obsolescence'. If they had read Japanese, they were given a special training course to learn German and subsequently posted to Kampala. If they were commercially brilliant, they were despatched where political expertise was the sole requirement. If they were geographers, they were given posts to advise on chicken diseases. It seemed as if, as soon as they had completed the long and arduous process of learning something, it was no longer required.[1]

The environment of the outsourcing contract is as subject to change as the general business environment in which the customer organization operates. Some flexibility in the provision of services may be built into the contract, but this will not always prevent other modifications being required or requested, perhaps to achieve a more effective result or to extend the scope of the services. A procedure for enabling variations to be made during the term of the outsourcing agreement needs to be established and agreed in advance so that it can be built into the contract, to enable the process of change to be controlled and the variations to be incorporated.

Both parties must be clear about who is entitled to instigate the change, whether there is a choice by either party in accepting or rejecting the change, and how control over the changes is to be maintained.

For an outsourcing contract entered into for obsolescent systems, a change control procedure will probably not be necessary. The contract will be for known requirements, to cover a limited period until the customer's replacement systems are up and running. Nor will it necessarily apply in the case of outsourcing contracts of limited scope for other reasons – for a single system or for a short duration. In other circumstances, however, the procedure for handling requests for changes should be part of the contract management processes.

Types of changes

The contract may categorize changes according to whether they are variations forming part of the normal service provision and included in the charges, or whether they should be dealt with by following the change control procedure.

Changes which may be implemented by the supplier in the ordinary course of events may include those concerned with improvements to the efficiency of the services, where the supplier has undertaken to do this over the term of the contract. The service charges may allow for an annual figure budgeted for resource effort in hours or days, which might be used for minor development work or for small modifications.

Changes which fall within the change control procedure may be those resulting from technological advances, amendments as a consequence of new legislation, new service requirements following a review of the services and changes arising from business strategy shifts.

The customer may seek changes for greater convenience, for economy or because of altered requirements. The supplier may be able to recommend efficiency or quality changes as a consequence of learning more about the customer's business and to take advantage of new technology. Most frequently, variations to the contract will mean relatively minor modifications to the services – for example, the number of reports which are required and by what deadline. The contract must not be so stringently drawn that it becomes difficult to make even these kinds of administrative amendment.

If changes are required to the terms of the contract itself, rather than to the substance of the services or the service levels or the technology, the procedure should be carefully controlled. The supplier and the customer representatives should not themselves have the power to amend the contract. This should be initiated by a recommendation made at a progress meeting and taken to senior management.

Technological, legislative and service-level changes

Access to advances in technology is one of the potential advantages of outsourcing. The supplier may have the option of achieving service-level objectives by bringing in upgrades in hardware, operating systems, software, advances in terms of processing power, storage capacity, new interfaces or communications networks. Alternatively, any proposed innovatory change may have to be subject to scrutiny through the change control procedure.

Variations in respect of which the customer has no choice may be necessary to cover revisions to standards or regulations and changes in the law as a result of new legislation or case law decisions. Payroll is one example of a system which requires constant attention each year or more frequently. Legislative modifications to taxes payable and taxable allowances must be incorporated. The amounts of salaries and wages paid will vary; volumes, in terms of numbers of staff being paid, amongst other matters, will fluctuate.

There are likely to be variations required to the service levels over the course of the contract term. Contractually, provision will be made for a periodic formal review of the services, leading to amendments which may be proposed by either the customer or the supplier.

Business strategy changes

The above are all examples of unexceptional changes within the service provision. Having entered into the outsourcing, the customer may be hoping to avoid major upheaval. Yet the possibility of enhancements and development, to bring about significant changes in the services, should not be discounted simply because such variations had not been foreseen when the contract was being negotiated.

Companies change direction, reorganize and rearrange their priorities. They strive to keep their competitive edge. They may do this by specializing or by diversifying, by restructuring management hierarchies, by looking outwards on a global basis or by cutting out non-core activities. Any of these activities will directly affect the IT resources they need and will be reflected in consequent changes to the way in which the outsourcing services are provided or to other aspects of the contract.

This may be so even where the contract is for a non-core application. For example, a company whose sales activities are primary may find that new regulatory activity by its business sector's controlling body means that the focus on order processing has changed and more information has to be supplied by law. There may be a close unavoidable deadline before the new systems have to be implemented. A company's ability to be first in the field may dramatically affect its profits. An order processing system may be precisely the sort of system which no one expected to revolutionize the business but which, as a result of the new regulations, is brought into the limelight.

For large companies, mergers and acquisitions have always caused problems for their IT departments. In some cases, they have not even gone ahead where the major strategic systems have been incompatible. This problem may be aggravated with outsourcing. On the other hand, outsourcing can provide a solution; information systems of a number of different subsidiary companies may all be outsourced to the same supplier until they can be amalgamated into one unified operation.

The procedure for bringing in changes

The change control procedure is part of the ongoing management liaison. It should be set out in detail in the contract.

Requests for changes may be put forward by either the supplier or the customer. Whatever the source of the proposal for variation, the supplier should carry out an evaluation of how long the proposed variation will take to implement, any likely costs for the customer – or any reduction in costs – and the effect on the rest of the services. In some instances, this may be carried out almost immediately by noting that there will be no effect on the services and that there will be no costs. However, an apparently trivial amendment may have many knock-on effects. A number of days should be allotted for the supplier to evaluate the impact of the proposed change on the level and standard of the services, what it would cost to implement, whether there will be any consequential savings, and to advise the customer accordingly in writing. Time limits may also be imposed for the customer to consider the supplier's evaluation and to agree the work and any associated costs.

In deciding whether the variation should be proceeded with, the customer may have no option – for instance, if it is required as the result of an error or if it is a legal imposition. There may need to be further negotiation over the speed of its introduction. The evaluation of the proposed variation will normally consist of whether it will constitute value for money and what the costs and difficulties of implementation will be if it is decided to proceed. Any change should continue to support the original objectives of the outsourcing and, indeed, benefit them. If additional staff are likely to be needed as a result of the proposed variations, the proposal may need to be discussed and senior management involved.

If it is agreed that the change should go ahead, a document, usually known as a change order, should be drawn up to set out the requirements, the costs and the timescale for the introduction. This document will serve to vary formally the service level agreement or the contractual terms if necessary.

The contract should make it clear whether the evaluation process is to be without charge as part of the supplier's general services. Depending on the method of charging, and perhaps on the nature of the proposed change, it would be typical for the supplier to accept the assessment of the change within its service provision. The return for the supplier will be in terms of the charges agreed for the work in carrying out the variation or for the extra work involved in its operation. If the supplier needs safeguards to ensure that it has sufficient resources at its disposal at the time that they will be required, then a suitably worded provision in the contract for adequate notice to be given of variations, for allowance to be made for recruitment and training, and for the supplier to choose when to implement the variation will provide protection against liability.

The change control procedure may involve a consultation process. However, there should be a requirement for the supplier to be reasonable in accepting a customer's request for variation and not to delay in proceeding with implementation. This will be important to the customer's control of its business, and in cases where there is no choice about introducing the amendment, such as the introduction of new legislation or upgrading hardware under the terms of a lease or supply agreement.

On the other hand, it should be the customer's right to refuse to accept any variation proposed by the supplier, whether or not there is an additional cost attached. The customer has contracted for a service to be provided for which it is paying. It must have the certainty of that service at the rates agreed. An argument which may be advanced to mitigate this is that the customer should take note of the outsourcer's concern, particularly in a wholesale outsourcing. If there is disagreement because the requirements of either party are unrealistic or because of a shortage of resources or budget, a dispute resolution procedure should be used and the matter escalated as discussed in Chapter 10.

Avoiding bureaucracy

The change control procedure is important for providing a structure to the sequence, substance, timing and discussion of proposed variations, so that both parties are aware of the implications. It will be necessary for the customer to know formally what the change will cost and to enable an assessment to be made of any additional costs and any effects on the rest of the outsourced systems, and when the change will take place. There may not be much choice with legislative changes, while there may not be any problem if frequency of report production is the issue. At the same time, the procedure must not be so bureaucratic that it will cause delay and result in it not being followed. The variation itself must always be documented and the service level agreements amended if necessary. This documentation should be kept with the contract as part of the contract administration. It may be helpful to number the changes. They should at least be dated and retained in chronological sequence or filed according to the part of the system which is affected by the variation.

If the procedure is not followed, discussions *after* the change has been effected about who is to pay or about the delays caused by its introduction and consequences for the rest of the system can become acrimonious.

The definition of the scope of the services should be clear on what is to be regarded as part of the normal service being undertaken by the supplier. This may include some additional work which would replicate similar general assistance provided to end users by an in-house IT department. However, a problem which may arise in practice is that the supplier's staff will often willingly carry out small variations free of charge beyond what is set out in the service level agreements, in order to keep the relationship with the customer happy and because, from their point of view, it seems a simple enough modification to implement. This raises the customer's expectations of what can be achieved for the price being paid. If in fact service-level performance is subsequently affected, then arguments ensue. In order to discourage this, the supplier must therefore ensure that its staff are subject to the disciplines of recording the variations. The supplier should always make it clear that any work for which there is to be no charge is not part of the agreed requirements – reserving the right to charge for other work.

Note

1   Alan Coren (1974), *The Sanity Inspector*, London: Coronet Books.

12 Confidentiality and security

Some types of business will require more sensitivity than others in the performance of the outsourcing services and the treatment of data and information. Broad statements made in the contract about confidentiality and security will demonstrate the general ethos which should apply to the outsourcing activities. Nevertheless, this is no substitute for identifying the areas for which specific assurances are important, to enable the contractual commitments to be precisely expressed. The identification process will form part of the customer's risk management strategy, in reviewing how secure in practice each of the systems and kinds of information for which the services are being provided should be, relatively or absolutely.

Long before negotiating the outsourcing contract, the importance of confidentiality arises at the preliminary stages of dealing with specialist consultants and potential suppliers. This is discussed in Chapter 3.

The contract itself should cover:

- confidentiality and integrity requirements
- obligations relating to personal data

- compliance, including compliance with security standards and with the requirements of standards and rules of regulatory bodies for certain financial systems
- restrictions imposed over access to premises, systems and data
- back up and disaster recovery procedures.

For safety critical systems there is a huge raft of additional considerations.

Confidentiality restrictions

Within the agreement there should be a provision to protect the customer's trade secrets and sensitive business information. If the supplier is working day-by-day at the customer's premises, it will be in a position to acquire information within the operational environment which is not for general circulation. What is discussed at the joint management meetings may concern future customer strategy and not be general knowledge. The customer may be able to detail the information which should be handled with special care, whether by its subject-matter or by its form – information about the structure of the business, financial data, customer lists, or whatever may be accessible to the supplier's staff. A standard confidentiality clause is likely to be taken less seriously than one which makes it clear what information does need to be treated with extra care and any special procedures which should be followed. The more distinctively the provision addresses the confidentiality requirement, the better the chances of its efficacy. The clause may extend to an express requirement for the supplier to keep its staff informed of what is to be regarded as confidential and to have special procedures for looking after the information, such as restrictions on its removal and instructions concerning its destruction. If the supplier will be using the services of third-party contractors who will be entitled to access confidential information, the supplier must take responsibility in the contract for their entering into confidentiality agreements which would be enforceable.

Confidentiality impositions will not all be one-way and wholly for the benefit of the customer. The supplier will also be anxious to protect any of its proprietary information, trade secrets and expertise which become accessible and available to the customer. However, the customer has to consider in advance how to manage the termination or expiry of the contract if it has become dependent on confidential information or proprietary methodologies belonging to the supplier. In the event of the supplier ceasing to provide the outsourcing services for any reason, the customer must have obtained a waiver of confidentiality for the purposes of being able to continue to run the services itself, or a licence to use the information concerned, or permission to pass the information on to a replacement supplier, so that the services will continue to be carried out.

The customer should be extremely wary in its response to any request to keep the terms of the outsourcing contract itself confidential. The customer would be severely constrained in the information it could legitimately pass on to third-party advisers or experts whom it might wish to consult if the outsourcing services prove unsatisfactory or increase in cost unexpectedly while the contract is in force, or in its negotiations with other potential suppliers when the contract is coming to an end.

The customer may be keen to restrict the supplier's ability to carry out outsourcing services for competitor companies in the same market sector. This may be perceived in terms of a potential or actual conflict of interest with its business, or a fear that expertise gained by the supplier from the customer's investment in outsourcing will benefit its rivals. This concern can be justified only if it is genuinely relevant. For example, if development services are being undertaken by the supplier for a new leading-edge system in conditions of utmost secrecy, a case may be established for the period over which the services are being provided. The supplier's agreement is likely to be gained only if the charges negotiated make it worth its while to limit its normal marketing and sales activities, and if the provision is expressed as narrowly and for as short a time as possible. This is also essential for the clause to be legally enforceable. It should be clearly justifiable and (subject to this) last ideally only for a restricted length on time from the commencement of the contract or, at a maximum, for the duration of the contract and possibly for a few months beyond the contract term. The business specialization should be identified for the contract as specifically as possible or, more effectively, the names agreed and listed of those direct competitor companies concerned. It would be preferable for it not to be a blanket exclusion, but rather that it should permit the supplier to act for the competitor company if the customer's consent is obtained in advance – if the situation were to arise. This is a more reasonable restriction and will enable the customer to assess at the appropriate time whether there will genuinely be any difficulties.

The supplier may want to publicize its association with its customer. This should not be permitted before the customer is ready for the arrangements to become public knowledge and at least the main contract terms agreed. The non-disclosure agreement in advance of the contract may need to cover this. A clause may be included in the outsourcing contract that any announcements or other publicity relating to the outsourcing services should be subject to the other party's agreement. If this is important for the supplier, the permission needs not only to be obtained but also to be communicated expeditiously; nor should it be unreasonably withheld or delayed, as timing is often significant – for example, in order to meet a press deadline.

These confidentiality requirements are mainly in terms of the relevance of the information to the customer or supplier's business. Legal considerations apply to the treatment of information which constitutes 'personal data'.

Treatment of personal data

'Personal data' is defined as being data held about living, identifiable individuals and has to be treated with greater care than other kinds of data. The object of data protection legislation[1] is to impose obligations on 'data users' who record and hold personal data by electronic means, concerning its collection, use, retention and disclosure, and to give concomitant rights to 'data subjects', who are those people about whom the personal data is held. There are certain exceptions – for example, for public security, defence and criminal law.

Data users have to be registered on the Data Protection Register and must follow eight data protection principles set out in the legislation[2] to ensure that the personal data should be held, processed and used properly, fairly and lawfully, that it is accurate and that there are adequate procedures for keeping it secure.

If the supplier will be managing and processing systems for a customer whose systems are in any way concerned with personal data, the supplier must be registered as a 'bureau' with the Data Protection Registrar for the purposes of the Act, and otherwise comply with the legislative provisions. A 'computer bureau' is defined more widely in the context of data protection than the term is normally understood. Here, it means those individuals or organizations providing services in respect of data which is electronically held or processed, in one of two ways. The first is by providing services in respect of data on behalf of other persons, where the data is processed by equipment operating automatically in response to instructions given for that purpose. This includes an intermediary who may not take any active part in the processing or may not necessarily have possession of a computer, if that party makes arrangements for the processing of personal data. The second is by allowing other persons the use of equipment actually controlled by the bureau for such processing of data.

The eighth data protection principle is especially relevant for bureaux. It states that: 'appropriate security measures shall be taken against unauthorised access to, or alteration, disclosure or destruction of, personal data and against accidental loss or destruction of personal data'.

Having registered as a bureau, the supplier should have a policy in place for personal data to be accessed only by those authorized to do so, for a legitimate purpose, and that if the data should be lost or destroyed, it will be able to be recovered without any harm suffered by the data subject.

The place where the data is kept is important and should have suitable security systems to prevent deliberate or accidental trespass. There should be no doubt about the reliability and integrity of the staff entitled to access the data. Genuine personal data should not be used for training, demonstration or development and testing purposes when fictional data could be used.

There are some exemptions from the requirement for registration. If the supplier is running a payroll system on behalf of its customer and the personal data is used *only* for calculating and paying wages and pensions, registration will not be necessary. However, the information must not also be used in any other way. Often it will be associated with personnel records or the records of purchases and sales for marketing purposes. Most exemptions are subject to stringent conditions. If there is any doubt, then registration is advisable.

The Data Protection Register is open to public inspection, and copies of entries can be obtained, so that a person can investigate whether personal information is being held about him or her. If damage has been caused by its unauthorized disclosure or if the person finds out that the information is inaccurate, or if appropriate security measures are lacking, that person is entitled to seek compensation through the courts. The data user may be criminally liable in failing to comply with the provisions of the Act.

A customer who is a data user must protect the personal data by ensuring that, in the outsourcing contract, at a minimum, the supplier confirms its registration as a bureau and its commitment to complying with the data protection principles and to any specific requirements for safeguarding the personal data. In particular, organizations such as those in financial services or direct marketing, whose businesses depend upon personal data, will need to be confident that there are sufficient security assurances in place.

The position on data protection in the UK is being modified, following a Directive on Data Protection[3] aimed at harmonizing the different data protection laws in the European Union. The Directive has extended the principles on which UK data protection legislation is based by referring to a right to 'privacy' for the data subject. The implication is that personal data must be treated differently from other data because of this fundamental individual right. No right of privacy as such exists in English law.

It is anticipated that the revisions to the legislation which will be required to be made under English law to bring the contents of the Directive into legal effect will enable increased flexibility and openness, such as a simplified approach to registration, taking into account the risks of processing and the nature of the data held. However, amongst other changes, in certain circumstances registration will extend to data held manually, where the records form part of a filing system.

By October 1998 all member states must conform to the Directive. A period of three years is to be allowed for transitional arrangements to be effected, and a timescale up to the year 2007 is permitted for implementing the requirements for those manual records which are included under the Directive.

Security

Breaches of security related to information systems are widespread. The 1996 National Computing Centre's Information Security Breaches Survey found lapses of various kinds, often involving significant costs and substantial impact. Computer viruses were the most common breach to be reported. Computer and chip theft had increased, and, in nearly one-third of such thefts reported to the survey, it took longer than a week for the organization to recover from its loss.

Thus there will almost inevitably be some attention to security issues in the contract, whether or not the outsourcing services cover sensitive business areas. The supplier may be asked to give a commitment to complying with the customer's own security rules. The contract may require the supplier to comply with external security standards, such as the purchase of ITSEC-certified products or British Standard 7799 for information security management.

'ITSEC' stands for IT Security and Evaluation Certificate Criteria. This is a joint venture between the DTI and the government's Communications Electronics Security Group, an authority for the evaluation of the security features of IT products and systems and the certification of the level of assurance. Products with ITSEC certification have gone through an independent testing and evaluation procedure in respect of errors and design faults related to security, and have achieved a defined level of information security.

BS7799 is a British Standard code of practice which is a methodology for security standards. It provides a basis for the organization of a security policy, in terms of personnel, physical and environmental security, computer and network management, system access, development and maintenance. It states that an organization should have a document which sets out its information security policy and allocates responsibilities both for information security and training and educating staff in security. Virus controls, data protection, business continuity planning, reporting of security incidents and compliance with the code are all covered.

The practical contractual provisions will encompass regular day-to-day security requirements, which will apply as a matter of course.

Where the outsourcing is carried out remotely, physical security on admission to the data centre may be a requirement.

Access to computer systems must always be properly authorized. This may be by means of a general authorization for the supplier in the contract. Any third-party contractors who need to access the systems should be given authorization entitlements within their consultancy service contracts with the supplier, in exchange for specific confidentiality obligations. Additionally there may be systems of password access and reinforcement of what is permitted by means of notices indicating copyright and stating that only permitted users have the right of access to the systems which appear on-screen at the time when the password is requested.

Contingency planning and disaster recovery

Contingency planning and disaster recovery procedures should also be available to enable normal services to be restored as soon as possible in the event of exceptional problems. If contingency plans already exist for the customer's information systems functions, these must be reviewed for their adequacy in an outsourcing situation. It is frequently the case, however, that the customer has not previously given serious attention to one-off catastrophes which could affect its systems capability. The process of deciding what procedures would be necessary and how they should be implemented would therefore need to be initiated as part of the contract preparations, ideally hand-in-hand with ascertaining the standards for the service levels.

Different degrees of back-up will be necessary, according to the importance of the particular system to the customer, to the priorities assessed by the customer, and on the length of time a system can be out of action without affecting the customer's business. For some systems, the result will be inconvenience only. For others – for example, where real-time processing affects business decisions – recovery must be immediate.

In the event of physical disaster striking the machines or the premises where the IT services are carried out, the supplier may be able to provide its own disaster recovery systems for critical systems at alternative sites of its own, or a separate disaster recovery contract may be agreed with a third party for temporary processing at a remote site. The manufacturer concerned may be able to help with schemes for replacement hardware. It may be that the services are provided at a number of customer sites and that there can be reciprocal fallback arrangements at a site which is unaffected by a disaster.

The contingency plan should therefore cover action plans for recovery to normal conditions following a disaster, once the extent of the damage has been assessed and actions prioritized depending on the relative criticality of the systems to the business. Provision for the supplier to test the contingency plan from time to time should be built in. The plan should be set out in terms agreed by both the supplier and the customer and incorporated into the contract. The supplier should then be able to give contractual assurances that the outsourcing services could be continued through any circumstances preventing normal operation, particularly for critical systems or services.

The risk for management is that the contract will focus exclusively on the normal operation of the outsourcing services and ignore practical confidentiality, security and contingency requirements. In considering the extent of security levels required, it should be borne in mind that the more rigorous are the security procedures and record-keeping required, the higher the costs will be. If the customer's existing arrangements are sufficiently effective they should remain in place, and the supplier should take on the responsibility for managing them.

Notes

1   Data Protection Act 1984.
2   Data Protection Act 1984, Schedule 1 – the Data Protection Principles.
3   Council Directive 95/46 on the Protection of Individuals in Relation to Personal Data (OJ 1995 L281/31).

13 Contract duration, termination and effects of termination

Outsourcing must be a finite arrangement, not an open-ended commitment. The decision on how long the contract should last is an important one. The contract may eventually expire or be renewed if the outsourcing supplier is willing to carry on providing the services, whether by renegotiation or on the existing basis. At this time the customer has the choice of inviting further tenders or bringing the work back in-house.

Whatever the outcome, continuity of the services must be ensured through contractual commitments, at all costs avoiding total dependence by the customer on the supplier – a situation known as 'lock in'.

Towards the end of the term, if the customer is comparing new bids for the work, the supplier will be expected to make available the relevant information about the services. If the outcome is that a different supplier or an in-house team is to take over the outsourcing, the handover by the supplier must include everything necessary for the service provision to be carried on, and the situation in respect of staff, equipment and software licences must be controlled.

Grounds on which the services may exceptionally be terminated early should be identified in the contract.

Looking ahead to the end

Most of the contract negotiations will be concerned with putting the framework in place, the transfer and management of resources and assets, the levels of service and the day-to-day operational practices once handover has taken place.

However, an outsourcing relationship is not a static affair and is part of a larger environment which itself is subject to change which may be subtle but will certainly be constant. During the course of the contract, the customer's business practices may be modified and its focus may consequently shift. Meanwhile, the supplier may be developing different strategies for gaining new work from its existing customers or it may acquire new customers which it finds more interesting for various reasons. Personnel on both sides will move on and be replaced. It is unsafe to assume permanence or predictability either in the relationship or in the services, and the duration of the contract will therefore almost always be for a fixed term.

How long should the contract last?

A small self-contained system or an obsolescent function may conveniently be outsourced for two or three years. The outsourcing of the whole IT function of a large company will more typically be for an initial term of between three and five years or longer, with options to continue and ongoing scope for variation.

Where the contract term is relatively short, charging rates may be linked to its duration, giving some certainty of income and expenditure for the supplier and customer respectively. The first increase in charges may then be imposed at the time when the contract term is due to be extended.

In a survey by Willcocks and Fitzgerald,[1] 95 per cent of the contracts were for four years or less. The climate of business uncertainty and growing awareness of supplier leverage are probably contributory factors to the shorter durations now being negotiated. How far can a company look ahead in this environment? How far ahead does its business plan extend? The evidence tends to show that it is the contracts of longer than five years which are likely to cause problems.

Nevertheless, ten- or twelve-year terms or longer are not unknown, particularly in the USA. For example, EDS contracted with Xerox for a ten-year, $3.2 billion contract in 1994 for the entire IT operations of Xerox worldwide, the largest outsourcing deal at that time.[2] This was followed by the Inland Revenue's widely promoted outsourcing transaction in the UK, again at ten years. In the UK there are some other long-term contracts – for example, the British Home Stores IT function, outsourced for 11 years. But these are the exceptions and well publicized as a result. For contracts of such long duration, a structure of formal checkpoints should be in place to review that the outsourcing is working consistently throughout the term, to build in scope for variations in the charges and to the services, and to set points at which negotiations may be reopened for particular aspects.

For an extensive and complex outsourcing, the customer will sometimes feel more secure if it instigates an initial transfer term of some months prior to a cutover date, on the principle that, if the supplier is not performing during that period as anticipated and agreed, the customer will then be able to terminate the contract early without having to pay compensation to the supplier. There may be other reasons why a short transfer period may be desirable – perhaps for administrative purposes to finalize the leases and asset transfers, or for working out service-level details. However, if it is not an intrinsic part of the transaction structure, a bedding-in trial period is likely to do no more than to provide a psychological benefit for the team or director ultimately responsible for negotiating the contract for the customer. If problems were to be encountered in practice in these first months of a large-scale contract, after expending so much energy in choosing the supplier and drawing up the contract, the whole worth of the extensive process of selection and negotiation would have to be open to question. The customer will look indecisive. The supplier will have to give business assurances in a wholly unsatisfactory atmosphere of uncertainty which is not conducive to long-term planning and a positive understanding.

Another alternative sometimes sought by the customer is for an entitlement to early termination despite the fixed term. In such an event, it would be necessary to build in a compensation payment to the supplier. On the basis that the supplier will be able to reallocate resources profitably elsewhere, the compensation will be payable only for the disruption attendant on the reallocation and for unrecoverable capital expenditure. However, the supplier may negotiate a more substantial payment if it has planned its resources' availability for the original term and is looking to cover its loss of profits.

Expiry, renewal or notice?

A set period for the outsourcing may be stipulated, at the end of which the contract will simply expire. For contracts which outsource the whole of the organization's IT, there may be provisions for the supplier to give early notice of its wish to renew and the terms on which it would do so and for the customer to respond. For less complicated, selective outsourcing, the term may be expressed as an 'initial period' and the contract would then have an automatic extension beyond the stated expiry date, normally on rolling 12-month terms unless notice of termination is given by either party, to expire at the end of the initial period or at an anniversary date.

There are three choices for the customer when the contract is drawing to a close, any of which may be more or less realistic according to the circumstances:

● to stay with the supplier on either the same or renegotiated terms

- to choose another supplier, preferably by going out to tender as part of the selection process, the current supplier being asked to retender
- to bring the work back in-house.

It is important for the customer to keep in mind, and plan for, the date when the contract will expire. It is easy to be caught out and then be forced into extending the original term by default, perhaps on unfavourable terms, having failed to prepare for a formal decision on whether to continue the relationship, renegotiate or set up internally.

The more complex the range of services, the more difficult it is to set up ways and means of ensuring a smooth transition to another supplier or back into the customer's organization. These are nevertheless likely outcomes for which to prepare. For example, in the survey quoted earlier, nearly one-third of outsourced organizations in the past five years ended the contracts rather than renewed them.[3] In half these cases, the terms were renegotiated; a further 28 per cent of cases involved a change of supplier; in 22 per cent, the IT work was brought back in-house. The findings of this survey were endorsed in an outsourcing survey published by *PA Consulting* in 1995. This survey found that 26 per cent of firms which had outsourced services subsequently decided that they would be bringing them back in-house. In further research, some companies found that they were so unhappy with their outsourcing supplier that they were prepared to pay to get out of the contract before its expiry, and chose to rebuild their in-house capability.[4] It was reported that the RAC brought network control functions which had been outsourced back in-house. This followed a change in the ways the networks were run, and the increasing significance of voice and data to its business.[5]

Thus, although it may seem, at the outset of the contract, that the whole purpose of outsourcing would be lost if it were necessary to visualize reconstituting the structure in-house at some future point in time, this is not an unlikely future scenario – and one which may not always be at the behest of the customer.

Although negotiations for renewal would normally begin well in advance of the date by which notice must be given, the notice period should be long enough for decisions to be taken about the future without unreasonable pressures. The customer needs time to renegotiate the contract terms and conditions, perhaps to organize a re-tendering process if the services are to continue to be outsourced, possibly to find a different supplier and transfer the services, or to arrange to bring the services back in-house. For its part, the supplier needs time to seek other sources of work if its services are likely to be terminated.

The customer must be alert to the date for formally giving notice so that the contract does not continue to run by default. Good contract administration procedures together with proper management liaison and reporting structures, as discussed in Chapter 10, will help the customer keep control of the timetable.

At the point of giving notice, the customer may reserve a right in the contract to call for an independent audit at its own expense, the supplier agreeing to provide without charge any information reasonably needed by the auditor. The aim of this exercise would be to establish objectively the levels of service being attained in relation to the charges, at this point in the contract life, for the purpose of comparing them against the original specification of services and service levels, in order to assess the value being obtained. This may be used as a rationale for staying with the supplier on similar or renegotiated terms, or as a basis for obtaining competitive quotes from third-party suppliers.

The supplier's continuing commitment

Towards the end of the contract term, the future relationship between supplier and customer will seem uncertain. The customer may be looking around at other outsourcing suppliers and requesting tenders, the current supplier being offered the opportunity to put in its own bid at the same time. Yet, at this time, the supplier will be in control of most of the information and know-how which would be critical to any other bidder.

The supplier should undertake to provide to the customer – or to the customer's representative if the customer is using the services of outsourcing consultants – the appropriate documentation, such as procedures, guides, third-party contracts and any additional information necessary to enable an effective re-tendering exercise to be carried out. This will enable potential bidders to quote charges which have taken all the relevant information into account. The supplier should be ready and willing to assist positively and constructively in providing assistance to the customer on matters relating to the services in the event of termination – even when its competitors will be involved – and to do its best towards a smooth service migration. The statement in the contract will be of a general nature. At the time the agreement is being negotiated, it will not be clear precisely what assistance will be helpful, nor for how long it will be needed. Some requirements will be clear from the start, such as retrieval or access of data in a suitable format and the continued operation of software, and these will be contractually specified.

The beginning of the relationship is the point at which the supplier should be at its most confident and optimistic about the ongoing quality of its services, and when the termination provisions can therefore most easily be negotiated. It will be most unsatisfactory to lay down principles of cooperation which should apply between the parties once the services have deteriorated, the relationship has broken down or the customer has found a more compatible supplier.

One lever which the customer may be able to take advantage of in this respect is the outsourcing supplier's reputation. The CSSA code of practice requires suppliers to provide all reasonable assistance on contract termination to transfer the provision of the services to the customer or to any third party nominated by the customer. If the supplier is a member of the CSSA, compliance with this code of practice should be contractually required.

As a safeguard, the customer may find it worth negotiating to allow for the services to be carried out on the same terms or on reasonable charges for a number of months beyond the date of termination, at its option. This is effectively a limited continuation of the contract, to which the supplier may not have any objection – unless it is about to enter into a more lucrative contract with another party!

The supplier must continue to respect the customer's security and confidentiality entitlements after termination.

Unless the supplier finds itself in the unhappy situation of wanting to extricate itself from the relationship – for example, if the services are being provided less profitably than it had calculated, or the work is not as interesting as it had hoped, or the systems are not expanding through further development as it had anticipated – the period prior to termination will be a difficult time. The effects of termination for a supplier who does not immediately have other sources of work will be severe, consisting of loss of profits and unemployed resources.

Continuity of human resources and use of assets

Where contracts are renewed or renegotiated but none of the staff originally involved is still around, the loss of corporate memory can become a serious problem. This can be more acute if the outsourcing has involved application systems – especially core systems and project management – rather than mainframe processing or operational networks.

The customer may consider negotiating a contractual right to approach the supplier's key staff or experienced personnel working on the contract – particularly any of the customer's former staff who had originally been transferred to the supplier – to provide continuity. (This would be an exception to any restraints which might be included in the contract on actively canvassing staff, as discussed at Chapter 6.) How far this could be successful in practice is another question. It would be entirely a matter for the individual personnel concerned. They cannot be forced to move or to return to a former employer, simply because they suddenly find themselves being considered as a desirable resource in the short term on account of their knowledge and experience. Moreover, it is likely that, during the contract term, at least some of the transferees will have been promoted to gain wider experience as part of a career structure within the outsourcing company or will have resigned to follow their own inclinations and will no longer work on the outsourcing services for their former employer.

All associated contracts, leases and licences, for equipment, software or other resources, must be investigated at termination for transfer, whether by assignment or novation, in the same way as at the commencement of outsourcing. A procedure should have been agreed in advance for recovering or re-purchasing appropriate hardware, with a formula for ascertaining the purchase price.

Licences for third-party software may need to be reassigned or novated. Where the supplier has used its own proprietary software in the service provision, and it cannot easily be replaced, on termination of the contract between the supplier and the customer a licence for its use must be made available to the customer or to the new outsourcing supplier, or the source code acquired. This too is a matter for negotiation by looking ahead. The customer cannot afford to permit the use of the supplier's own software if it is indispensable to the service provision and there are no ways of being able to use it after the end of the contract.

Exit management plan

A provision should be included in the contract for a termination, or 'exit management', plan to be drawn up. This will cover all the activities needed in the transfer of the services from the supplier so that their migration back to the customer in-house or to another supplier can be carried out as seamlessly as possible in an atmosphere which is likely to be tense. At best, the provisions should be applicable in whatever circumstances of termination arise.

It may include the following: a list of processes for managing the transition; the job titles of those vested with authority for dealing with the various elements; the resources which will be called on; a plan for communicating with staff of both parties, and with third-party suppliers and customers; and an outline programme for transfers, assignments or novations of assets, licences of intellectual property rights and any other contracts relating to the provision of services. The transition tasks should be kept independent of the normal service delivery process to avoid any danger of the service provision being compromised.

It is a matter for negotiation as to who should prepare the exit management plan, and at whose cost. It may be offered by the supplier, as part of the overall services, and agreed by the customer. Ideally, it should be drawn up before the contract comes into effect, but this is a counsel of perfection and it is more realistic to set a fixed period in the contract, such as 120 days from the date the contract commences, for it to be compiled and agreed.

It should be recognized that any exit management plan drafted at an early stage of the contract relationship is going to be in outline and incomplete. In a long-term arrangement it is in the customer's interests to keep the plan up-to-date and to formally review it from time to time; formal arrangements for doing this should be included in the contract. The customer may also require a review of the adequacy and currency of the plan to be included in its internal audit regime.

Reasons for early termination

The right to early termination before the contract has run its full course may be caused by breakdown of the relationship following breach of contract, or by either party's change of status, insolvency or imminent insolvency. The risks associated with the supplier's financial instability may be limited by such devices as escrow arrangements (discussed in Chapter 8), or guarantees from parent companies. It would be practical for the customer to get to know those individuals familiar with the services who would need employment if their employer ceased to exist.

A termination by the customer on account of breach of contract may be caused by the number or seriousness of breaches of service levels by the supplier or by fundamental financial, technical or organizational problems in the provision of the services. The supplier will require the ability to terminate if there are continuing problems concerning payment by the customer or difficulties preventing it from carrying out the services.

If the management procedures in the contract are working effectively, any problem should first be dealt with through the escalation procedures as discussed in Chapter 10. The termination provision will be resorted to only if these procedures fail to produce effective results.

Early termination is not a right to exercise lightly. It will cause all sorts of problems for both parties but it may calculate to be the lesser evil where the alternative is to let an inadequate service continue. The customer always has to balance the costs in terms of accepting disappointing services against the costs of terminating through breach on this account. This is an intrinsic difficulty in termination. Bringing in another company meanwhile would not only be expensive for the customer – whichever party would ultimately be found responsible, whether this would be a deficient supplier or an aggrieved customer – but, in the short term, would not be possible without considerable disruption. There will also be the expense of temporary contract staff, together with the extra efforts which would have to be made by senior management.

A provision may be included to give either party the opportunity of making amends before the final drastic right of termination is invoked. It would be reasonable to allow a period of grace, say 30 days, to give the supplier a final chance of improving its performance. Similarly, before the supplier terminates for non-payment, the customer should be advised that, if payment has not been received within a number of days, termination would be the consequence. Negotiation should be carried out with the customer's objective in sight, and it may be that payment of a reasonable sum to the supplier for, say, the transfer of data and continued licensing of the software, may enable the relationship to decline in a more cooperative manner.

The contractual right to terminate for breach of contract, may be limited to 'material' or 'substantial' breach, to avoid the contract being ended precipitously. The customer may exercise this right if the supplier is not meeting its contractual obligations – that is, where the service is consistently not being carried out effectively so that service levels are not being met or there is other negligence such that internal remedies and escalation procedures will not work.

On termination by giving contractual notice there is no obligation for reasons to be given. But where termination is on grounds of breach of contract, a dispute is almost inevitable and the reason being given is likely to be challenged.

The customer should ensure that terms are included in the contract to require the services to be continued by the supplier in the event of disagreement. The supplier must not have the contractual right to suspend or withdraw services if there is conflict. One US court case concerned a dispute over termination where an outsourcer had simply switched off a bank's system as a negotiating tactic. It was held that this had not violated the relevant computer misuse laws because the contract left the supplier with the right to do this. While not suggesting that the same result would necessarily occur in the UK, it makes sense for the customer to include an appropriate term in the contract, to cover this.

The supplier may be prepared to agree to continue to provide the services if the non-paying customer is willing to make its normal payments into a third-party stakeholder account, rather than fail to pay and being in breach of contract itself.

When there is so much effort being invested in choosing a satisfactory supplier and in agreeing the service levels and other terms of the contract, it can be difficult for the customer to remember that the association with the supplier is not bound to be permanent. Yet it is essential to articulate the exit routes clearly at the time the contract is being negotiated, when both parties can dispassionately agree the ways of bringing the contract to an end, the related procedures planned and the details elaborated.

Notes

1 Leslie P. Willcocks and Guy Fitzgerald (1994), *A Business Guide to Outsourcing IT*, Business Intelligence Limited.
2 Reported in *Computer Business Review*, April 1995.
3 Willcocks and Fitzgerald, *op. cit.*
4 Lacity and Hirschheim (1993), 'The Information Systems Outsourcing Bandwagon', *Sloan Management Review*, Fall 1993.
5 *Computer Weekly*, 29 May 1997.

14 Redressing fault and failure

In addition to setting out the functions and responsibilities of the parties, the outsourcing contract will state the level of commercial and legal risk accepted by each party in the transaction. How much risk can each party afford to bear?

At the time of drawing up and negotiating the contract, the problems that might arise in the operation of the outsourcing services should be envisaged. The mechanisms for controlling them will be elaborated and agreed. During negotiations, a priority is to find ways of avoiding and minimizing risk as far as possible, of allocating risk between the parties, and of managing risk in operating the contract. There must be adequate control techniques in place to enable the customer to maintain at least the basic services in the event of the supplier's failure or delay, or on termination of the contract. Following this, agreement must be reached as to what limits of liability are acceptable.

Some risks will legitimately be excluded under the contract. For example, the supplier may exclude any liability for failing to meet the time laid down for production of a report where this depends upon input from end users which did not arrive by the stipulated deadline. Other contractual provisions will govern the extent to which liability will be acceptable, such as a financial limit dictated by the supplier's insurance cover. At law, however, the parties are not free to contract entirely on their own terms, or entirely on those of the more powerful party, in respect of limiting or excluding liability.

What happens if anything does go wrong? Continuing failure by the supplier to meet service levels or failure by the customer to make payments at the agreed times are examples of breaches of obligations in the contract. Administrative procedures for monitoring the contract will help to control the risks. Failure to meet the critical service levels may lead to pre-agreed compensation payments. The innocent party will attempt to enforce the contract. If the dispute cannot be averted, it must be resolved. If escalation procedures and informal negotiation processes do not succeed, there may have to be recourse to formal adjudication.

The party at fault will be liable for damage suffered by the other party, to the extent agreed in the contract, or as settled through negotiation, or as decided by the courts or other means of dispute resolution. 'Retrieving a contract that goes wrong is more expensive and difficult than you would imagine; this is true even when there are termination clauses in place in the original contract.'[1]

What can go wrong for the customer?

The customer will try to protect itself against the risks that the services contracted for will not be provided adequately, and that the supplier's performance does not meet the anticipated standards.

Throughout the chapters of this book, individual risks in outsourcing for the customer are discussed from the perspective of avoiding the risk or limiting the damage by means of the contract. The principal risks include: hidden costs or escalating costs; loss of control by the customer over its strategic use of IT; the supplier's confident claims of competence when bidding for the work not being fulfilled in practice; performance which deteriorates over time; and lock-in to the contract.

The difficulty in practice for the customer is to know at what stage to take the decision to end the relationship and terminate the contract when performance has sharply or consistently worsened. The business must be kept running, and there must be provisions in the agreement to facilitate this. It is not in the customer's interests to rush into legal proceedings as soon as a problem arises, yet there may come a point when the contract has to be enforced.

What can go wrong for the supplier?

The fear of risk is not all one-sided. Suppliers are in the commercial business of outsourcing and must ensure that payment is commensurate both with what is being offered and making a reasonable profit. Mechanisms for payment will be included in the contract for the supplier's benefit. If there is any genuine difficulty or extended delay on the part of the customer in meeting the payment, the supplier must have the right to suspend or terminate the contract.

Beyond these requirements, the supplier will use the contract to limit its liability arising from work undertaken under the contract to a reasonable extent compatible with the scope and nature of the work undertaken.

The supplier's view of risk allocation is to ensure that it will not be held responsible for any faults which it has not caused. Actions, delays or omissions by end users, other contractors or the customer itself may have led to the problem. However, the customer may argue that the risk belongs to the business which the supplier is taking over and, on this interpretation, there is no reason why the consequences of another contractor's failure should not be borne as much by the supplier as by the customer.

Failure without fault

Not all deficiencies in the performance of a contract will be attributable to the fault of one or both of the parties. Historically, in law, it used to be the case that if a promise were to be made, in a contract, then it absolutely bound the party making it, however the circumstances surrounding the performance of the contract might change. Over time, case law developed from this uncompromising position to permit the contract to be brought to an end without blame attaching to either party, if it became impossible for the contractual obligations to be performed. In these circumstances, the contract is said to be 'frustrated'. All sums paid will be recoverable and no further sums will fall due.

However, this applies only within very narrow limits – to a fundamental failure, beyond the parties' control, which creates a situation radically different from the original expectations. For example, the contract would be frustrated if its whole purpose was for something to be done which was subsequently prohibited by an Act of Parliament changing the law, *before* the purpose was effected.

Causes beyond the reasonable control of either of the parties, which prevent performance once the contract is in force, such as freak weather conditions or terrorist activities, are referred to as *force majeure*. Delay or failure during the contract's operation in carrying out its obligations due to reasons of *force majeure* will not constitute legal frustration. To protect a party from being liable on the occurrence of these kinds of causes, many contracts include a standard provision which suspends the contract during the *force majeure* conditions. To allow some certainty to be imposed on an unsatisfactory situation, the provision may give either party the right to terminate if the situation continues for a defined period of time, perhaps 90 days.

A *force majeure* clause gives both parties the confidence that they can abandon the contractual requirements if either of them is constrained by events over which it is powerless. While performance is suspended due to the *force majeure* reasons, the party unable to carry out its obligations will not be in breach.

It may be helpful for the wording of the clause to specify causes which, if left unstated, could stimulate arguments as to whether they should genuinely fall under the *force majeure* umbrella. Industrial action affecting either party may or may not be regarded as justifying non-performance; fundamental damage to hardware, however caused, may be considered in a similar light.

Although the clause is often inserted automatically in many kinds of contracts, for an outsourcing contract which includes disaster recovery, and where reliance is being placed on the delivery of a service within highly constrained parameters, a customer should reflect on what would ever constitute a failure by the supplier to perform being reasonable, especially if there are comprehensive contingency obligations. The provision may therefore be excluded or suitably restricted.

Conditions, warranties and indemnities

The customer will expect the supplier to give various warranties and indemnities to confirm its levels of commitment. A warranty is a term of the contract which is less important in principle than a condition. The term does not have to be expressly stated as being either a warranty or a condition. Whether a term of the contract is a condition or a warranty depends on the parties' intentions at the time of making the contract. The difference has implications for the remedy available to the innocent party.

A *condition* is of such primary importance to the contract that, if it is not realized, the whole transaction is fundamentally affected. The contract will be repudiated and damages may be claimed by the injured party. An outsourcing contract may have a condition requiring financial guarantees from a parent company or consents from third-party licensors to be procured by the supplier by a particular date (there would have to have been some practical reason for the contract to have been executed before obtaining these guarantees or consents). If the condition is not met by the date specified, the contract will be discharged.

Breach of a *warranty* given by one party will entitle the other party to claim damages under the contract. For example, a supplier may warrant that if its nominated service manager leaves the post, his or her replacement will have similar levels of training, experience and expertise, and the approval of the customer will first be sought. If there is a breach of this warranty and the customer suffers quantifiable loss as a result, a claim for damages may be made.

An *indemnity* is compensation for loss suffered. Indemnities may be contractually offered by either party, normally for specific circumstances and often subject to upper financial limits. The supplier may agree in the contract to indemnify the customer in respect of losses caused by its non-compliance with legislation, intellectual property rights infringement of software as discussed in Chapter 8, damage caused in using the customer's premises, or failure to comply with the exit management plan as referred to in Chapter 13. The customer may indemnify the supplier in respect of copyright infringement of its own software and for any losses arising from staff transfer.

Limiting liability

The ideal position for the supplier would be a total exclusion of liability arising from any of its activities under the contract.

The ideal position for the customer would be for the supplier to give an indemnity against all the losses and liabilities arising from breach of its obligations under the contract.

Yet it would be unrealistic for any supplier to contract either for no liability or for unlimited liability. The contract will therefore reflect a compromise. The supplier cannot afford to leave itself exposed to compensation for all and any of the customer's unforeseeable losses and for which it is highly unlikely to obtain insurance cover at all, or for which cover is available only at a very high price. The supplier will therefore place a limit on its liability. If protection is required, the customer may have to look to its own insurance or, alternatively, ask the supplier to take out extra cover for which the costs will (at least in part) be passed on to the customer. This is, after all, the last resort. The customer should be confident in its choice of supplier and, through continuous review and management of the service being provided, should be in a position to arrest most problems at an early stage before they escalate.

The law prohibits liability being excluded or unreasonably limited under certain conditions. If one of the parties is a consumer, or if the contract consists of standard terms of business, liability *cannot* be restricted for breach of contract unless it is 'reasonable' to do so.[2] A party can count as a 'consumer' for the purposes of this legislation if it is not dealing in the course of business, and a company taking outsourcing services may be defined as a consumer on this basis.

'Reasonable' is a term now found in much legislation and has to be interpreted in relation to the facts of the case. In deciding on whether a contractual term is reasonable, the factors taken into account will include: the relative bargaining position of the parties; any inducement to agree to the terms; and the availability of insurance to the parties. The overall context of the contract will be reviewed if this is necessary to determine what is reasonable.

Typical clauses in outsourcing contracts will state that liability causing death or personal injury from negligence will not be excluded or limited, as if this were a positive feature – although it would normally be unlikely to arise. It would not in fact be legitimate to exclude or limit such liability. Similarly, liability arising from negligence for damage to tangible property caused by negligence cannot be excluded, and should therefore be accepted by the supplier subject to a reasonable limit. These liabilities would normally be covered under the supplier's public liability insurance.

Further provisions will be a matter for negotiation. The supplier will endeavour to limit its risk – perhaps to a specified sum under its professional indemnity insurance or to the value of the contract – which the customer should resist. From the customer's point of view, potential losses result from the damage suffered if the system goes wrong. The risk is therefore not necessarily directly referable to the price being paid.

The supplier ought to be carrying some insurance cover for certain events, as an important back-up to the contractual relationship. The supplier will never want to find itself in a situation where, even if it has failed to carry out its part of the contract, the resulting liability is so great as to wipe out all its profits or even to put it out of business. This will not help the customer either.

It follows that any financial limit of liability specified in the contract should not be arbitrary. It should be justifiable by the supplier, in terms of the type of business, the level of risk to either party, the insurance cover, the value and importance of the contract and the level of the supplier's turnover.[3] A figure which cannot be defended in these ways will not be regarded as reasonable by the court in applying the legislation, and therefore cannot be relied on to limit liability for breach of contract, even if it is stated in the contract.

Recoverable losses

The remedy for the party suffering loss is in terms of financial compensation or damages for the direct losses which are foreseeable at the time of entering into the contract. Such losses are those arising in the ordinary course of events from the breach of contract or 'as may reasonably be supposed to be in the contemplation of both parties at the time they made the contract as the probable result of the breach of it'.[4] At the time the contract is made, the supplier and customer will not be expecting any breaches to occur. What is intended by 'contemplation' is that, if the breach had been considered as a possibility at the time of entering into the agreement, it would have been concluded that there was a serious likelihood that the loss or damage – that is, the disadvantage suffered – was likely to arise as a result.

For losses to be recoverable by compensation, they must either arise naturally from the breach of contract or be those which could reasonably be anticipated by both parties to occur if the performance of the contract should fail. Direct damage or loss will be covered but normally other kinds of loss or damage, described as consequential or indirect, will be categorically excluded in the contract. Reference is sometimes found to 'special damages' being excluded. This is an ambiguous term, usually relating to identifiable damage in personal injury cases, and therefore not appropriate to outsourcing.

What is 'direct' loss or damage? Wasted expenditure has been held to be a direct loss in a case involving a failed computer system.[5] It included support and testing payments, payments to consultants, the cost of wasted computer stationery and the cost of wasted management time. A shortfall in income and associated interest caused by software error will also be recoverable. On the other hand, loss of data is not normally defined as a direct loss.

Loss of profits would not necessarily be directly recoverable unless the customer had drawn to the supplier's attention in advance that this would be a direct result of a failure in the outsourcing arrangements. For a single system or service, the losses may be confinable. For wholesale outsourcing, if things went wrong, then loss of customer profits would be highly likely to be a direct consequence, particularly if the outsourcing included mission-critical systems. 'Economic' loss is often contractually excluded from the scope of liability. Yet losses suffered by a company are most likely to be economic.

One contracting party will not necessarily be fully aware of all the business activities of the other, and of their relative priorities. The customer should be sure to advise the supplier, during the negotiations, of the probable losses which would result if the contract were breached. The losses will then be foreseeable in the context of the outsourcing, and the supplier will be made aware that they matter to the customer.

It is up to the customer to recognize in advance what its financial risks would be if the contract should go wrong, and to communicate these to the supplier. The earlier the contractual process is initiated, the more time the parties will have to consider how best to manage them by forward planning as far as possible.

If the matter came to court, judicial discretion might be the arbiter in the decision as to what would be included as the customer's direct losses for which the supplier would be liable. One commentator has said: 'If the judge thinks that justice requires the plaintiff to be compensated, he will suggest that the loss or damage suffered was likely. If not, he will say that it was too remote'.[6]

Compensation, not penalty

The legal principle under English contract law to compensate for breach of contract is to try to put the party not at fault into the position it would have been in if the contract had been carried out. It follows that the injured party should not benefit by making a gain which is over and above its actual loss. It is not able to penalize the party at fault, by expecting to receive an arbitrary or an excessive sum of money if the contract is not fulfilled. Any provision in the contract with this objective will not be legally enforceable. Along with this principle is one known as 'mitigation' in that the innocent party is expected to attempt to mitigate or minimize the loss caused, rather than to take advantage of its position.

A claim for damages for work badly done would therefore typically be for what it had actually cost to have the work carried out or put right by a third party, but no more than this.

A genuine effort beforehand may be made to estimate certain losses which would arise in the event of a particular breach, and to include this provision in the contract as 'liquidated' damages, meaning the fixed amount which has been calculated. If it is impossible to estimate the potential loss precisely, then the most convincing figure in the circumstances should be agreed of the losses likely to be suffered which would be recoverable at law. Different sums may be set for different breaches. Chapter 5 discusses liquidated damages as a remedy for service level breaches. A liquidated damages provision means that the parties are aware of the extent of liability and their risks under the contract.

If the consequences of the breach make this kind of calculation almost impossible to estimate in advance, some kind of decision has to be taken between the parties for what the customer would be prepared to accept and the supplier prepared to concede, which would be acceptable as a bargain made between the parties.

This imposes some limit on what might be payable to the injured party. As far as the actual figures are concerned, if the loss turns out to be less than the estimate, the pre-agreed figure will apply. The parties are regarded at law as free to negotiate and agree a figure to represent liquidated and ascertained damages provided that the figure does not constitute a penalty. The risk to the customer is that the agreed amount turns out not to be sufficient compensation if the breach of contract and consequent losses are sustained. Conversely, it can be to the supplier's advantage to have a liquidated damages clause in the contract.

However, the supplier's risk is that it would not affect the amount of liquidated damages if, at the time of breach of contract, the customer was not in fact suffering any loss, provided that the estimate had been properly calculated. It is therefore important that the customer be able to justify the reasoning behind any figures. If there were to be a dispute, the supplier is immediately likely to challenge the figure representing the liquidated damages, and to seek to discover how the figure has been worked out. If the sum had been satisfactorily calculated and agreed in the first place, the supplier's case would be very weak.

The amount may be expressed in the contract for purposes of compensation and not intended as a penalty but, if it is in fact a penalty, it does not matter what name it has been given. A single lump sum stated as being payable by way of compensation on the occurrence of one or more or all of several events, with various outcomes of damage, would be presumed to be a penalty. If the liquidated damages figure varies simply by growing in line with the contract value or the supplier's increasing workload, this too would be unlikely on the face of it to be a real estimate in advance. Any amount stated in terms of a percentage of the contract sum runs the risk of not being enforceable. Percentages will give rise to arbitrary figures. It is not obviously logical to relate in this way the value of the contract to potential loss suffered. If the provision were to be held to be a penalty, then the customer would not be deprived of the right to claim for damages, but would have to prove the loss suffered.

Compensation independent of contract

Beyond the contract, one of the parties may be liable in what is known at law as 'tort', a branch of law separate from contract, applying to certain unauthorized acts, or in some cases omissions, causing damage. One example of a tort is defamation (libel or slander). Another is negligence. The party making the claim of negligence, the plaintiff, would have to prove that the party against whom the claim is made, the defendant, owed it a *duty of care* – a particular legal term for defining the extent of responsibility for damaging acts (or omissions) – that there was a breach of that duty of care, and that the breach caused the damage. The relationship between the plaintiff and defendant is not automatically going to involve a duty of care. Where it does arise, phrased in legal terms, is where the plaintiff is so directly and closely affected by the defendant's acts or omissions that the defendant should have considered the possibility of harm caused to the plaintiff. The damages will be measured as the loss caused by the act or default. The defendant will be liable for any loss arising directly and naturally, which was reasonably foreseeable at the date the act or default took place.

It is possible for liability to exist in tort at the same time as in contract. The fact that the parties have a contract does not in itself prevent there being liability in tort, if this is not excluded under the terms of the contract. For instance, there may be an obligation, whether specified or implied in the contract, to take reasonable skill and care. Apart from the contract, there may in any case be a duty of care for the other party to take reasonable skill and care not to be negligent in a broader situation than the scope of the contract itself, perhaps where additional services are carried out.

It would be possible to claim for economic loss independently of the contract as a result of statements made by the defendant, such as loss caused by advice negligently given or misinformation negligently stated, provided that the negligence in making the statement could be proved, that the defendant knew that the statement would be communicated to the plaintiff, and that the plaintiff, would be relying on it as expert knowledge or professional expertise for the purposes of entering into the transaction. This might affect either the supplier or the customer.

However, negligent liability other than in contract is subject to some restrictions at law. Claims for economic loss are extremely limited in scope, and it is difficult to predict the situations in which they would have any chance of success. Damages may be recovered in tort for economic loss resulting from negligence only in very narrow circumstances. The defendant must have special knowledge and skill and assume responsibility towards the plaintiff. The plaintiff's economic loss must have been caused by negligence of the defendant in misusing the specialist expertise claimed. The plaintiff must prove reliance on this special knowledge and skill. Normally, however, any expectations of expertise between the parties will be set out in the outsourcing contract which will be the source of any legal proceedings.

Commercially, claims in negligence tend to be more expensive to pursue and more difficult technically than claims in contract, and the outcome more uncertain to predict. In a commercial relationship the contract will be the focus. Legal actions based on contract in outsourcing disputes are more common than actions brought under tort.

Resolving differences

Negotiating a good contract is the best safeguard against disputes arising which cannot be readily sorted out. Terms for dispute prevention should be built into the contract, through controlled procedures for the provision of information, communication, reporting structures and decision-making.

Nevertheless, in any close, complex and lasting commercial relationship, differences and disputes are almost inevitable. Methods for handling them should ideally be agreed at the time the contract is being negotiated. Having these techniques set out in the contract itself will save time, trouble and expense later.

Yet disagreements over what is acceptable, genuine differences of expectations and divergence of opinions or approaches are almost inevitable in the performance of complex contracts. Some of the potential difficulties arising have been discussed in earlier chapters. The aim must be to deal with these difficulties before they harden into disputes. Sometimes this will mean unenforceable 'agreements to agree' – for example, when the scope of service level agreements has to be detailed in the course of operating the services. Any software development process must have its own checkpoints. Change control procedures must allow for assessment of any changes to be imposed. No commercially-driven agreement of this nature can anticipate all possible contingencies or be totally unambiguous.

Failure to meet service levels and disagreement over a variation to the services may each call for remedies of different orders. The overriding objective is to be able to solve the problem to the mutual satisfaction of both parties quickly and with minimal disruption and costs. This will not always be achievable.

Where there is evidence of non-compliance with service levels and performance requirements, recompense can be provided for automatically, as discussed earlier in this chapter and in Chapter 5, through a scale of compensation for liquidated damages or service credits associated with payments due, together with action taken to put matters right.

By moving up the decision-making hierarchy, escalation procedures for discussion and problem resolution can be built into the normal management of the contract, as detailed at Chapter 10, to assist in overcoming deadlock. It is often the case that senior managers who are remote from the day-to-day operations will bring a fresh approach to resolving issues.

A final level of escalation procedure within the control of the parties themselves alone may be contractually provided for by requiring an extraordinary management meeting to be called with the aim of resolving differences and maintaining the relationship, to be attended by a small number of senior named representatives of each side.

Another possibility is to bring in an agreed external independent technical expert for referral of certain kinds of disputes of a technical nature – given that the disputing parties can at least agree both on the choice of such a person whose professional verdict they will each accept, and also on what constitutes a dispute confined to technical issues. This can be a relatively quick, informal and flexible way of reaching a decision.

Termination is a final sanction. Even here, a last opportunity for negotiations may be a contractual requirement so that the party intending to terminate will have to give a number of days' notification – typically at least one month, expressed as 20 working days – before the termination takes effect. Again, this is an opportunity for further discussion and negotiations in the hope of finding a solution to avoid bringing the relationship to an end.

Taking formal action

If the dispute is not resolved by any of the methods discussed above, or if other informal means of negotiation fail, then formal methods of dispute resolution need to be implemented, whether Alternative Dispute Resolution (ADR), arbitration or formal legal court proceedings – that is, litigation. If ADR or arbitration is agreed at the time of negotiating the contract to be suitable, this should be included as a contractual term.

While formal means of dispute resolution are in progress, the customer may be unwilling to pay the supplier. The contract may set out terms for an interest-bearing deposit account to be set up in a bank in the names of both parties so that the customer may continue to comply with its obligations in the contract, but the payments will be made into this account. Following resolution of the dispute, the sum in the account, together with accrued interest, can be paid out according to what was determined by the proceedings.

Alternative dispute resolution

The idea of mediation and conciliation in commercial relationships is not new, but ADR is an umbrella term for an approach which formalizes these concepts. It stresses each party's own responsibility for voluntary negotiation for the purpose of settling disputes in a non-binding context. Introduced in the last few years as a new procedure, it may be invoked as an alternative to litigation or it can be brought in at any stage in the litigation process. The procedure can be halted without further obligation or commitment at the behest of either party. Even if the mediation is not successful in the ultimate resolution of the dispute, it may reduce the number or the complexity of the issues concerned.

There are a number of ADR options which can be modified as required by the parties, and which can range from informal conciliation to consideration of the issues by a third party in a mini-trial format. The basis is that an independent neutral third party will be appointed by, or on behalf of, the parties in dispute, who will not be a decision-making adjudicator but a facilitator acting with the active consent of both parties, trained to guide the parties themselves to reach a negotiated and perhaps creative compromise. Experts may participate. It is important to a successful outcome that the facilitator is skilled and able to avoid any appearance of bias. Some legal and technical advisers are trained in ADR, although it is not necessary to have any particular formal qualifications to become a facilitator. It is also important that the representatives of the parties which are involved in the process have authority to settle on behalf of their organizations.

Because ADR is voluntary, the parties do not have to agree in advance to be bound by the outcome; in fact it may be explicitly stated that they do not need so to agree. However, it is reasonable to state in the contract that the parties should agree to treat as binding any agreement once it has been concluded. The position concerning costs should be clarified – for example, that each party will bear its own costs incurred in taking part and equally share the facilitator's costs. A time limit may be contractually imposed in order to prevent ADR being misused as a delaying tactic.

Information gained in the course of the mediation, such as weaknesses which are learned about the other party's case, could subsequently be exploited in subsequent litigation, if the ADR is not successful. A mediator will normally be required as part of the ADR instructions not to pass on confidential information. There should also be a provision that the negotiations themselves should be conducted in confidence without prejudice to the parties' rights in legal proceedings. The parties may thereby have to agree not to introduce certain material revealed by the ADR procedures into subsequent arbitral or judicial proceedings – for instance, any opinions about the basis for the settlement facilitated by the conciliator or mediator. Reference to a failed ADR process conducted on a formal 'without prejudice' basis will not be permitted in subsequent litigation. Care must be taken in drafting the ADR clause, to ensure that the implications are covered and understood.

Lord Woolf's recent report on the civil litigation system[7] has recommended that the courts encourage alternatives to the resolution of disputes in legal proceedings. In the Commercial Court, some procedural requirements have been amended so that parties have the opportunity of considering ADR, allowing for adjournments and extensions of time to this end.

ADR is certainly worth considering where both parties appreciate that a continuation of their working relationship is desirable: where there are points in favour of each side's case; where the underlying business interests of each party are clear; where each party is genuinely ready to listen to the other side of the argument; and where both parties are clear that they wish to avoid the high costs of litigation or arbitration. Its value lies in the chance of achieving an early settlement cheaply by responsiveness to the parties' needs. Although it may be used at any stage of a dispute, and as an adjunct during the course of litigation or arbitration, it would normally be the first recourse of the parties. If there are ADR provisions in the contract, then that procedure must first be invoked before initiating legal proceedings through the courts. If the parties agree on this route, one good reason for putting it in the contract is to avoid any appearance to the other party of weakness by suggesting it at the time the dispute arises.

It is not automatically the best route to follow and, in certain instances, such as alleged fraud or where there are novel or important points of law, it will not be appropriate. Cases concerned with legal principles will still require legal adjudication processes. The success of certain remedies at law, such as injunctions which are discussed later in this chapter, may be inhibited if action is not taken early because ADR was tried and failed. Settlements agreed through the ADR process are not so easily enforceable as a court judgment.

More is written about ADR in theory than appears to happen in practice. Because the outcomes are agreed by the participating parties to be confidential, success stories are not publicized. There is a point of view that continuing negotiation with a view to early settlement is a characteristic of the English litigation processes and does not need separate treatment by means of ADR.

If the parties cannot agree on, or do not know of, a mediator, a named organization can be appointed in the contract to select one, such as the British Computer Society or the Centre for Dispute Resolution (CEDR), one of a number of independent organizations set up to handle disputes which fail to be resolved through ADR. Its scheme for IT disputes is linked with the CSSA. The addresses of these organizations are set out in Chapter 15.

Arbitration

For many decades, and especially since the end of the nine-teenth century, arbitration has been an important form of formal dispute resolution. The City of London is world-famous as a first-class commercial arbitration centre.

Arbitration is an adversarial process with an impartial arbitrator – or possibly more than one arbitrator in highly complex and high value disputes – selected by or on behalf of the parties, who will adjudicate by making a decision or an award. It has a framework of formal rules, but the procedures are more adaptable than in litigation because the arbitration tribunal is appointed to deal with a single dispute.

Arbitrators' powers depend on the legal jurisdiction and the procedural rules of the parties. In the UK, a new Arbitration Act[8] sets out the scope of arbitration proceedings and the powers of the arbitrator. The Act is based on the main principles of resolving disputes impartially, avoiding delay and expense as far as possible, providing essential safeguards, and auton-omy for the parties in making choices about the methods to be adopted. The powers of arbitrators have been strengthened and the role of the court consequently restricted. The few man-datory provisions are limited, relating to such matters as the enforcement of a ruling or an award made by the arbitrator. Otherwise, the parties are free to make their own arrangements for conducting the arbitration. If there is no agreement about procedure made between the parties, the arbitrator is given wide powers to decide on the conduct of the arbitration, evidence and procedure.

The scope of arbitration therefore lies within the control of the parties. Terms can be set out in advance in the contract, to define where the arbitration is to be held, rules of evidence and formalities of procedure which will apply. The parties can control the timing of the hearing. Whereas a case listed for hearing in court will have to join the queue for a date which may be months or years ahead, the parties can appoint an arbitrator or a team of arbitrators who have no backlog of cases or other commitments and who will be available within a short space of time.

A decision made by the arbitrator will be final and binding on the parties and cannot be appealed, unless it can be shown to be wrong in law or that the arbitrator acted in bad faith.

Arbitration proceedings take place in private. There are occasions when one or the other party may consider that publicity would be a useful lever in negotiating a dispute. However, maintaining the confidentiality of the process, by avoiding public denigration and loss of reputation, may be helpful to the parties.

An arbitrator must be found who is acceptable to both sides, with expertise concerning the area in dispute and sound knowledge about arbitration procedures. If the parties fail to agree on an arbitrator within a number of days, the contract should nominate the chief officer of a suitable organization, such as the Law Society, the Society for Computers and Law, the Institute for the Management of Information Systems, or the British Computer Society, to make the selection. The Chartered Institute of Arbitrators is the professional organization for arbitrators. The addresses for these organizations are set out at the back of this book.

Arbitration should not be accepted automatically as a means of dispute resolution without appreciating the implications in relation to costs, lack of publicity and choice of arbitrator. The arbitrator's fees must be paid and, even if the matter is settled beforehand, the arbitrator may nevertheless be entitled to some payment. A neutral location for the arbitration proceedings must be found and paid for.

An arbitrator has no power to bring in a party who was not party to the original agreement to arbitrate without their consent. If other parties are likely to be involved, litigation will be a more practical means of dispute resolution.

Litigation

Whenever there is a dispute, the parties to a contract may go to court. Legal action must normally be initiated within six years of the date of the breach of contract, or if the breach was fraudulently hidden, six years from when it was discovered. This time limit is known as the limitation period. Some suppliers will negotiate for this legal entitlement to be restricted contractually, to two or three years, on the grounds that this gives a reasonable period of time for formal action to be initiated, makes it more feasible to collate the evidence relating to the breach and makes their own forward planning and insurance assessment easier.

For contracts executed as deeds, the limitation period is 12 years. Although it is not necessary for outsourcing contracts to be deeds, some organizations, such as local authorities, have standing orders requiring major contracts to be executed in the form of deeds, and this extended limitation period will be one of the consequences.

To succeed in a civil case in court, the plaintiff must prove that it has suffered damage caused by the defendant's breach of contract, on the balance of probabilities. Proving and quantifying the breach can be difficult and complicated. Over the length of time, which may extend to a number of years, which litigation may take in proceeding from the issue of proceedings to a court hearing, the parties will have many chances of reaching a settlement, and most cases do in fact settle without a court hearing.

Under English law, the risks for litigants if a case proceeds to court include an obligation for the loser to pay a large proportion of the winner's legal costs, as well as its own. Litigants will take into account the mounting costs as the litigation proceeds as well as the business case which they were originally fighting. Costs may exceed the damages being claimed. This can act as an incentive towards settlement.

Injunctions

The law recognizes that damages would not inevitably be an appropriate remedy for wrong suffered, where the timespan involved from issuing proceedings to the court action in itself would contribute to further wrong.

For example, if confidential information had been publicized in breach of a non-disclosure agreement, or if software has been copied in breach of its licence, the damage would have been done. What is required is to prevent the wrongful action being repeated.

An injunction or an order for specific performance is a discretionary remedy which may be ordered at the discretion of the court to stop a breach of contract or to require some positive act to be carried out in accordance with the contract. An interlocutory injunction may be applied for as an emergency remedy before the court hearing of the full issues relating to the case.

The remedy is 'discretionary' in that the court is not obliged to grant it automatically. In reaching a decision, the court will have regard to the state of affairs surrounding the matter. The standard of conduct of the parties making the application to the court will be relevant to the court's consideration. If the application had not been made promptly, or if the applicant was also acting wrongfully under the contract, this would be regarded adversely and the application would probably fail. Again, the court may take the view that damages awarded after a full hearing would be adequate compensation and that an injunction is not necessary, so that the application would not succeed.

It is a basic tenet of English justice that an order by the courts should be made only after the defendant has had an opportunity of presenting a case. The exception to this is where it appears that the applicant will suffer injustice because of delay or action by the respondent. An application for an injunction may then be made urgently *ex parte* – which means without the presence at the hearing of the party who is the respondent. If this exceptional condition applies, the court will then consider whether any damage might be suffered by the respondent through inability to present its case. An applicant may have to give an undertaking to compensate the respondent if, at the full hearing, the case were eventually to go against the applicant. The respondent could be compensated for the interim decision under the undertaking given by the applicant. If compensation cannot be awarded, then the risk of the applicant losing must be outweighed by the risk of injustice to the applicant in deciding on the need for the respondent's presence at the interim hearing. Once the order is made, the respondent should be informed without delay to give him the chance of arguing the case at court.

Thus, in software piracy, if a respondent knew that an applicant was taking proceedings, there would be a temptation to destroy the evidence by removing the software from the computer system. Prompt action *ex parte* by an applicant may be the only means of obtaining an effective result.

Notes

1 Leslie P. Willcocks and Guy Fitzgerald (1994), *A Business Guide to Outsourcing IT*, Business Intelligence Limited.
2 The Unfair Contracts Terms Act 1977.
3 Ibid.
4 *Hadley* v. *Baxendale* (1854) 9 Ex.341, restated and refined in later cases.
5 *Salvage Association* v. *CAP Financial Services Limited* [1995] FSR 654.
6 Michael Whinney in *New Law Journal*, 27 March 1992.
7 Lord Woolf (1996), *Access to Justice: The Final Report*, London: HMSO.
8 Arbitration Act 1996.

15   Conclusion

In conclusion, then, here are some of the main points to watch out for in the outsourcing contract. One possible structure of headings for the services agreement and the business transfer, together with the schedules which may be needed, is proposed; this may serve as a checklist and reminder of the issues which have to be addressed.

So, what are the main lessons to be learned? First and foremost a customer's existing IT problem will not be successfully solved merely by outsourcing. Certainly there are outsourcing suppliers who will be willing and capable of taking over a customer's IT facilities and services in an unsatisfactory state and improving them. This will be an effective means of overcoming the problems within contained costings only where the customer is making a positive contribution in planning for, and creating, the contract, and in having ongoing review processes in place. The customer must retain control of the strategic direction of the contract. If there are no suitable internal resources, this control may have to be achieved by buying in consultancy expertise from a source with no interest in providing any prospective outsourcing service itself.

Lack of preparatory work by the customer and the imposition of an unrealistically short timetable will not provide the groundwork for a successful outsourcing contract. A customer/ supplier mismatch is less likely to occur if the customer's preliminary investigations into its outsourcing requirements and searches for the appropriate supplier have been carried out wisely. As with any system procurement, badly defined service requirements cause hidden costs. A supplier who does not understand the customer's business will not provide the service required.

Customers will be more likely to select the best supplier for what they want and negotiate a successful outsourcing contract if they are aware of their priorities, whether these are primarily: a focus on the core business; better utilization of in-house staff; flexibility of IT response; better-quality service; or cost savings.

Outsourcing is characteristically selective rather than wholesale, taking on average a quarter of a company's IT budget. Selective outsourcing is more likely to meet a customer's expectations and will carry less risk than total outsourcing. The wholesale outsourcings that are so newsworthy are actually atypical.

The contract should be clear and understandable, and ideally will be a pragmatic working document, setting out the details of the particular arrangements. Through the drafting and negotiating of acceptable terms, it is the principal means of managing the legal risks in outsourcing and – once it has been executed – in managing, monitoring and measuring the services. It facilitates the business planning and implementation for balancing the rights and responsibilities of both parties so that they can work together.

Thus the ground must be prepared, the supplier selected and the staff issues managed. If, in spite of this, the outsourcing becomes an outright failure, the terms of the contract must be enforced, by termination if necessary, and alternative arrangements made.

Contract structure

Here is one suggested format for the services agreement and the business transfer agreement.

Services agreement

Introductory provisions
- The Parties:
  Names and addresses of the customer and the outsourcing provider
- Recitals:
  A brief note on the purposes and background of the Agreement, conventionally set out in two or three paragraphs
- Execution:
  The signatures of the parties may appear here or at the end of the Agreement
- Definitions used in the contract

Commercial provisions
- Duration of contract
- Services – preparatory services if appropriate
- Requirements to meet service levels
- Supplier responsibilities
- Customer responsibilities
- Charging provisions and payment terms
- Accommodation
- Intellectual property and software licensing
- Management control and representatives
- Key employees
- Change control
- Contract variations

Security
- Confidentiality
- Publicity and public announcements
- Audit requirements
- Contingency planning and disaster recovery

Levels of risk
- Warranties
- Indemnities and limits of liability
- Liquidated damages

Termination
- Termination for cause
- Effects of termination
- Assistance on termination
- Exit management plan

General provisions, including:
- Entire agreement
  What has been agreed, not extraneous documents or verbal agreements
- Assignment
  Whether assignment to another party is permissible
- Severability
  If one provision is ineffective, this will not affect the remaining terms
- Waiver
  If a breach is not enforced at any time, this does not affect its subsequent enforceability
- Notices
  Formal notices to be in writing and provisions as to acceptability
- Governing law and dispute resolution procedures

Attached contracts, schedules and agreements
- Business transfer agreement
- Scope of services
- Service level agreements
- Hardware details
- Software details
- Staff details
- Charges details

- Management liaison details
- Client policies
- Disaster recovery provisions

Business transfer agreement
- Definitions and interpretations
- Sale and purchase
- Assets included in the transfer
- Taxes
- Completion
- Apportionments and prepayments
- Conduct between commencement date and cutover
- Employees
- Third-party contracts
- Warranties
- Costs and stamp duty
- Further assurance and assistance
- Confidential information
- Limits on liability
- Access to retained records and assistance with disputes
- Announcements and publicity

General provisions (see services agreement format) including:
- Entire agreement
- Assignment
- Severability
- Waiver
- Notices
- Governing law and dispute resolution

Attached contracts, schedules and agreements
- Assets
- Employment details
- Property agreements
- Third-party contracts
- Pensions

Addresses of organizations mentioned

British Academy of Experts
2 South Square
Gray's Inn
London WC1R 5HP
Tel: 0171 637 0333

**British Computer Society
(BCS)**
1 Sanford Street
Swindon
Wiltshire SN1 1HJ
Tel: 01793 417417
Fax: 01793 480270

Business & Technology
magazine
19 Bolsover Street
London W1P 7HJ

**Centre for Dispute
Resolution (CEDR)**
Princes House
95 Gresham Street
London EC2V 7NA
Tel: 0171 481 4441

**Chartered Institute of
Arbitrators**
24 Angel Gate
London EC1V 2RS
Tel: 0171 837 4483

**Commission of the European
Communities**
Main office in Brussels:
Rue de la Loi 200
B-1049, Brussels

Tel: 0032 2295 1111
Fax: 0032 2295 0281
UK Office:
Jean Monnet House
8 Storey's Gate
London SW1P 3AT
Tel: 0171 973 1992
Fax: 0171 973 1900

**Computer Economics
Limited**
51 Portland Road
Kingston upon Thames
Surrey KT1 2SH
Tel: 0181 549 8726
Fax: 0181 541 5705

Computer Weekly **magazine**
Quadrant House
The Quadrant
Sutton
Surrey SM2 5AS
Tel: 0181 652 3500
Fax: 0181 652 8923

Computing **magazine**
32–34 Broadwick Street
London W1A 2HG
Tel: 0171 316 9000
Fax: 0171 316 9160

**Computing Services and
Software Association (CSSA)**
Hanover House
73 High Holborn
London WC1V 6LE

Tel: 0171 405 2171
Fax: 0171 404 4119

Institute for Internal Auditors
13 Abbeville Mews
88 Clapham Park Road
London SW4 7BX

Institute for the Management of Information Systems (IMIS)
Edgington Way
Ruxley Corner
Sidcup
Kent DA14 5HR
Tel: 0181 308 0747
Fax: 0181 308 0604

Law Society of England and Wales
113 Chancery Lane
London WC2A 1PL
Tel: 0171 242 1222

National Computing Centre (NCC)
Oxford House
Oxford Road
Manchester M1 7ED
Tel: 0161 228 6333
Fax: 0161 236 8049

Office of the Data Protection Register
Springfield House
Water Lane
Wilmslow
Cheshire SK9 5AK
Tel: 01625 535277

Official Journal of the European Union
The Office of Official Publications of the European Communities
2 rue Mercier
L-2985 Luxembourg
Fax: 00 352 292942759

Salary Survey Publications
10 Gwyn's Piece
Lambourn
Berks RG16 7YZ
Tel: 01488 72705

Society for Computers and Law (SCL)
10 Hurle Crescent
Clifton
Bristol BS8 2TA
Tel: 0117 923 7393
Fax: 0117 923 9305

Tenders Electronic Daily **(TED)**
ECHO
Customer Services
BT 2373
L-1023 Luxembourg

UK IT Security Evaluation and Certification Scheme (ITSEC)
Certification Body
PO Box 152
Cheltenham
Gloucestershire GL52 5UF
Tel: 01242 238739

The VAR Journal
19 Bolsover Street
London W1P 7HJ
Tel: 0171 917 7794
Fax: 0171 323 0708

Selective bibliography on outsourcing

CBI (1997), *Outsourcing IT – A Real Business Guide* (ed. Stuart Rock), London: Caspian Publishing Limited.

Cooke, Ken (1996), *Outsourcing*, London: Institute of Chartered Accountants (IT Faculty).

Institute of Directors and IBM (1993), *Director's Guide to Outsourcing IT* (ed. Stuart Rock), London: The Director Publications Ltd.

Klinger, Paul and Burnett, Rachel (1994), *Drafting and Negotiating Computer Contracts*, London: Butterworths.

Lacity, Mary C., Willcocks, Leslie P. and Feeny, David F. (1995), *KPMG Impact Programme – Best Practice Guidelines for Outsourcing*, London: HMSO.

Lacity, Mary C., Willcocks, Leslie P. and Feeny, David F. (1995), 'IT Outsourcing: Maximise Flexibility and Control', *Havard Business Review*, May–June.

Lacity, Mary C., Willcocks, Leslie P. and Feeny, David F. (1996), *Best Practices in Information Technology Outsourcing*, Oxford Executive Research Briefing, Oxford: Templeton College.

White, Robert and James, Barry (1996), *The Outsourcing Manual*, Aldershot: Gower.

Willcocks Leslie P. and Fitzgerald, Guy (1994), *A Business Guide to Outsourcing IT*, London: Business Intelligence Limited.

Woolf, Lord (1996) *Access to Justice: The Final Report*, London: HMSO.

In the trade press, *Computer Weekly*, *Computing* and *Business Technology* regularly cover reports and analysis of anecdotes, current transactions and disputes concerning outsourcing. They will often report on surveys carried out specifically on outsourcing, or on general surveys on IT strategy and expenditure, which have results relating to outsourcing.

Legislation references

As this is not an academic textbook nor a closely reasoned legal textbook, general legal references only are given.

Acts
Arbitration Act 1996
Copyright Designs and Patents Act 1988
Data Protection Act 1984
Misrepresentation Act 1967
Supply of Goods and Services Act 1982
Trade Union Reform and Employment Rights Act 1993
Unfair Contract Terms Act 1977

Directives
Acquired Rights Directive 1977 (77/187/EEC) ('on the approximation of the laws of Member States relating to the safeguarding of employees' rights in the event of transfers of undertakings, businesses or parts of businesses' ('ARD')
Compliance Directive (86/665/EEC)
Consolidated Utilities Directive Co-ordinating Procedures of Entities Operating in the Excluded Sectors (water, energy, transport and telecommunications) (OJ 1993 L 99/84)
Council Directive 95/46 on the Protection of Individuals in Relation to Personal Data (OJ 1995 L281/31)
Services Directive (92/50/EEC)
Software Directive: Directive on the Legal Protection of Computer Programs 91/250 EEC OJ 1991, L122/42.
Utilities Remedies Directive (92/13/EEC)

Regulations
Collective Redundancies and Transfer of Undertakings (Protection of Employment) (Amendment) Regulations 1995 (SI 1995 No 2587)
Copyright (Computer Programs) Regulations 1992 (SI 1992 No 3233)
Public Services Contract Regulations 1993 (SI 1993 No 3228)
Transfer of Undertakings (Protection of Employment) Regulations 1981 ('TUPE')
Utilities Contracts Regulations 1996 (SI 1996 No 2911)

Index